MORALITY AND THE SELF

Library of Philosophy and Logic

General Editors:
P. T. Geach, J. L. Mackie, P. F. Strawson, David Wiggins,
Peter Winch

IDENTITY AND SPATIO-TEMPORAL
CONTINUITY
DAVID WIGGINS

THE LOGIC OF POWER
INGMAR PÖRN

CATEGORIAL FRAMEWORKS
STEPHAN KÖRNER

REASONS FOR ACTIONS
RICHARD NORMAN

COUNTERFACTUALS
DAVID LEWIS

FORM AND CONTENT
BERNARD HARRISON

METAPHYSICS AND ESSENCE
MICHAEL A. SLOTE

MORALITY AND THE SELF

MICHAEL WESTON

OXFORD
BASIL BLACKWELL
1975

ISBN 0 631 15700 X

Printed in Great Britain by
Western Printing Services Ltd, Bristol
and bound at the Kemp Hall Bindery, Oxford

Contents

Acknowledgements

Most of the work for this essay was done at King's College, London, for the degree of M.Phil. My thanks are due to Professor Peter Winch, who provided encouragement and criticism both at that time and subsequently.

1. Morality and Purposive Action

The idea that the notion of purpose is central to that of human action has long provided the background against which philosophical thought about morality has operated. Given such a background it has often seemed as if there were only two possible ways in which moral considerations can enter into what a man does or into his thoughts about his actions: as means to his goals, or as goals themselves. As the purpose of this book is to cast doubt on both such moves, I want first to look at this paradigm for the understanding of action and thought about it, and the role it allows for morality.[1]

1. THE PARADIGM

We often ask people why they are doing, have done, or are going to do, certain actions, and what they say in reply is usually said to be, or to form part of, their reasons for performing those actions. Of course, they may lie or not be aware

---

[1] The use of such a paradigm and the provision of such a role is found in both the contemporary developments in Anglo-Saxon moral philosophy exemplified in the writings of Hare and Foot. It is unnecessary to establish this in detail in the light of the conclusions by these writers, which I consider below, that morality is either a means of mediation between conflicting desires or the specification of those things a man needs if he is to want any thing.

of their reasons, but the paradigmatic case of having and giving one's reasons provides the necessary contrast for these anomalous cases. The paradigm of purposive action places restrictions on the kind of statement which can be called a 'reason for action' and provides a model for the form of connection between these reasons and what is done. In brief, the 'reason' takes the form of a statement of fact, which becomes a 'reason' in so far as that fact has weight with the actor in the pursuit of a goal. The fact is connected to the goal as it concerns what may or must be done for its achievement, and is connected with the agent's actions because to want the goal is, in the usual case, to will whatever brings its attainment.

Within this account, the giving of reasons for an action takes the following form:
'Why are you doing A?'
'Because doing A is a means to Gi'
'Why do you want Gi?'
'Because it is a means to Gii'.
But somewhere this string of reasons must come to an end, and in so far as 'giving reasons for actions' is a matter of specifying means to goals, reason-giving stops when one specifies certain goals which are not themselves a means to anything further. The agent's relation to these goals is generally accommodated in the formulae 'X wants G for its own sake' or 'X just wants G'. Clearly, anything the agent himself gives as 'reasons' for pursuing the goal cannot be assimilated to the account of the reasons he has for wanting to do, or to have what makes possible, actions directed towards the goal. Yet, of course, people do say things, and often a good deal, in answer to the question why they pursue the ends they do. What the paradigm rightly indicates is that such 'reasons' cannot take the form 'because A is a means to B'. Hence his model of purposive action requires an account for two kinds of 'reasons':
(a) Those which are answers to the questions 'Why are you

doing A/Why do you want T?' of the form 'Because it is a means to G'.
(b) Those which are answers to the question 'Why do you pursue G?' and which take a non-instrumental form.

The necessity for the latter kind of 'reason-giving' is sometimes blurred by the assumption that the final 'reason' in the chain is of the form 'I just want G'. Whatever the status of such remarks, it is clearly not the same as those 'I want' statements occurring lower down the chain, where reasons for wanting can be given in terms of the connection of what one intends to do with the achievement of an end. Either, therefore, 'I just want X' is the only form of 'reason' which can be given to the final question of the kind 'Why do you want X?', or another form of reason giving, although not one consisting of the specification of an end to which the subject of the question is a means, must be admitted. And it seems we meet such reason-giving when people say 'what they see' in some particular goal or activity they pursue. However, as the conception of such reasons and the associated idea of 'seeing' something in what one does has played no role in the development of an account of morality within the purposive paradigm, I leave its consideration until the next chapter.

Reasons of type (a) take the form of statements of fact: that x is a means to y is my reason for doing x (if x specifies some action) or for bringing about x (if x specifies some condition conducive to y's attainment). Obviously enough, not all such statements of fact are in fact reasons: they become reasons for action only if one wants the end specified. Hence, we arrive at the distinction between a *possible* reason and a *reason for* a particular agent. Thus, that x is a means to y is a possible reason for doing x if one wants y, and that x is a means to y becomes a reason for me if I want y and know that x is a means to it. The latter class allows for the distinction between having a reason and acting because of it in terms of the domination of one desire by another. Given that

I want y I have reason to do x, but given that doing x is incompatible with doing z, for which I have reason wanting a, I may do z and not x if I want a more than I want y. Such are the prospects for an account of conflict and decision within the paradigm.

This scheme provides two possible accounts of a change, decline or development, in what an agent does. He may (i) acquire new knowledge of ways to achieve his goals, or lose that which he has, or (ii) acquire new goals and/or lose old ones. The latter possibility has received little attention, although our notion of reasons of type (b) above could help us provide an account of the surely important process of 'coming to see something' in an activity or goal, and of 'no longer seeing' anything in one. More often, the theories assume as given the desires for the goals, and answer the question of a change in the agent's pursuit of them in terms of an increase or loss of knowledge of the appropriate means. (Although even within this restricted perspective, the problem of giving an account of the process of 'losing interest in' something can hardly be raised, for it is not equivalent to that of forgetting how to do it.) This account has unduly restricted the notion of learning which can be accommodated within such theories, for it tends to lead to an assumption of certain fundamental, and hence non-acquired, desires underlying the process of learning. Learning then tends to be equated with gaining the knowledge to satisfy the desires. Such accounts, however, are not often explicitly stated, for moral philosophers lack interest in processes of change and development. Hare, however, provides an exception (*LM* pp. 62–3).[2] For Hare, learning to do something is learning how to perform acts of a certain kind in a certain type of situation. This he terms 'learning a principle'. We accept the principle initially, and, in the face of different circumstances, either modify it or

[2] In what follows, page references to *The Language of Morals* are prefixed *LM*, and those to *Freedom and Reason FR*.

leave it alone. Both the initial acceptance of the principle and the decision to alter or maintain it require a reference to effects which we desire. Learning is a process of coming to know facts of the form 'if you do a then b will result'. One accepts the principle if one wants b, and one alters or maintains it according as a in fact does or does not bring b. For this tale to get started, it would seem, the desire for b must be presupposed. If this is not the conclusion we should arrive at, the theory owes us an account of how we acquire the desires that we evidently do.

Just as moral change is assimilated to change in one's knowledge of facts of the form 'if you do a then b will result', so the problems one may face because of one's possession of the notions associated with purposive action, are read as technical ones. One may not know how to achieve b, or which out of various possible routes is likely to be the most effective. And here we can locate the role of the helpful observer or technical adviser. In so far as we are all technicians of the satisfaction of desires for goals, knowledge of the means to those goals is potentially common property. Hare's example of the novice driver is appropriate here (*LM* p. 63). A man who has driven in many different kinds of situation is experienced, in the sense of having a wide knowledge of possible road and traffic conditions and their effects on the achievement of safe travel. Many things will be second nature to him which would be difficult or impossible for the beginner. However, the experienced driver may give advice to the novice, for there is no reason why what is good for one in any given driving condition should not be good for the other. Either driver has the same goals, and hence the more experienced in their achievement can tell the novice the best means for their production. A man who has much experience of driving in icy conditions may tell someone who has little how to avoid skidding or how to remedy the situation if one does, and so forth. The inexperienced will either take notice or find out for himself. In this context he can find out what the other found in the past, for the problems posed by their possession of certain goals are the same for both.

2. MORALITY WITHIN THE PARADIGM

That moral considerations are important to people has posed a continuing problem for moral philosophy, and that this importance is often emphasized through a distinction between the moral on the one hand and the merely prudential on the other would seem to pose an obstacle for any assimilation of moral to purposive language. The economy of the model is preserved, however, in locating morality's role in connection with certain peculiarly important desires, thereby, at a stroke, both providing the required assimilation and explaining the importance of moral considerations. I want to look now at this move, and see what sort of distinction it provides between the ideas of prudence and morality.

As is so often the case the important move lies in what the problem is taken to be. Moral judgements are construed as answers to the question 'What shall I do?' The problem moral philosophy must solve is how they can possibly provide such answers, and this problem takes the form of the question: what reasons could one have for paying attention to moral considerations? As the only 'reasons' that are considered possible issue from the purposive paradigm, the game is lost before it is properly begun. But with what results?

We noted above Hare's account of learning. Learning to act is learning to do certain things in certain kinds of situation because to do so has certain consequences for the agent's desires. Consequently, these desires are presupposed by the account of learning, and this applies equally to the moral case. 'When in our early days, we are given our elementary moral instruction, there are some things we are told and some things we do. If when we did as we were told, the total effects of our so doing, when they happened, were always such as we would not have chosen had we known, then we should seek better advice, or, if prevented from so doing either work out our own salvation or become moral defectives.' (*LM* p. 71) In other words, unless their obeying certain moral principles resulted in satisfying certain of their desires, people would not learn them; as the principles are learnt, they must, therefore, be productive. Once again, the individual's desires are presupposed by the operation of morality. This leaves one with the alternative, in distinguishing morality from prudence, either of merely labelling certain desires as 'moral' (e.g. a man's most dominant ones) or of locating the difference in the operation of morality on preformed, purposive projects. In the former account, morality would concern certain of the goals a man has, in the latter the means taken by him to gain his goals. Hare takes the latter course.

He attempts the distinction between morality and prudence through the notion of 'universalizability'. This is glossed by Hare as 'possibility of giving reasons' and finds its natural habitat within his discussion of 'meaning'. Whenever we use a word, we are told, we commit ourselves to using it in any case (or allowing it to be used in any case) which shares the relevant features with the case of our initial use. The universalizability of 'red', for example, consists in the fact that 'red' is correctly applied to objects having a certain feature in common, which featured can be given as the 'reason' for applying the word in their case. Moral words contain a descriptive element, and, because of their action-guiding role, an additional feature. If we explain a moral term M by a universal rule 'All things with features a, b, c are M' our explanation seems to run parallel with that of any purely descriptive word, 'All things with features f, g, h are D.' However, as the moral term is action-guiding, its application in any case will recommend (or advise against) certain actions. As such, the universal rule becomes, not just a rule for the correct application of the word, but a principle of conduct. And this means that its use by someone assumes that he has accepted it, and hence that the effects of such acceptance are consonant with the pursuit of his desires. Thus, someone is misusing a descriptive word if he applies it where the features specified in the meaning rule are not present, but so to apply a moral word shows not a misuse, but an acceptance of different principles of conduct.

However, in this form the idea of universalizability will hardly provide the distinction between the obviously prudential and the moral. The metamorphosis of the meaning rule into a principle of conduct must surely go for any sort of term which is action-guiding, and this includes prudential terms ('effective', 'good', 'best' and so on, used of means to ends) as well as many aesthetic and religious ones as well ('beautiful', 'holy' etc.). And if this is the case no distinction will have been drawn between morals on the one hand, and aesthetics, religion or prudence on the other.

Hare, however, makes the peculiar claim that this property of universalizability carries with it the implication that any moral judgement I make about my own case commits me to a similar judgement about any similar one, even if these latter involve not myself but other people. Hence, the sense of 'similar' here excludes the possibility of counting the fact that this case is my own and that is not as a relevant difference. Hare seems to think that this follows from the original account of universalizability, but it can hardly do this since that account applies to any words that have a meaning, and in a particular sense to action-guiding ones. The universalizability of prudential judgements, for example, lies in the fact that if x is a good means to y, then anyone who wants y has thereby a good reason to do x. For it to be a good reason for someone it is necessary only for x to in fact be a good means to y, and for that person to want y. But, of course, when I say

'I ought to do x as it leads to y', although it is true, that I, having a desire for y, regard myself and anyone whatever who wants y as having thereby a good reason to do x, I do not predicate my saying 'I ought' on my being able to want anyone whatever to want y. On the contrary, often I especially do not want others to want what I do: when I am buying a piece of sculpture for my collection, for example. The universalizability of prudential judgements, therefore, lies solely in their having reasons which would be reasons for anyone else who desired a particular goal. Hence, merely from the notion of universalizability we cannot conclude, as Hare wishes to, that when I morally say 'I ought' I predicate my saying this on my ability to accept anyone whatever acting as I intend to do. Such a conclusion does not follow from the notion of a 'reason' as such, but must rather mark the difference between what it is to have a moral and a prudential reason for doing something. But if it does not follow from the idea of universalizability itself, it must be established in some other way, and it is difficult to see how this could be done in the light of moral examples where 'I ought' is used but any implications for what other people ought to do denied. (We shall meet such a case in chapter 3 when I discuss the central event of Conrad's novel *Lord Jim*.) Indeed, it would seem impossible on such a view to make sense of the moral distinction between a man who considers others in deciding what to do himself, and the arrogant man who follows his decision 'I ought to x' by 'so anyone ought in this position'. (I am not intruding a personal moral viewpoint here. The point is, this is a possible and recognizably *moral* distinction, and as such one for moral philosophy to articulate, not deny. To deny it would be to intrude a personal moral view.)

The absence of a perspective to accommodate such a distinction in this account is emphasized when we realize that the peculiarity of the universalizability of moral judgements we have noted is not to be accepted as a brute fact about moral

B

as opposed to prudential discourse, but as a fact having a point *within* prudence. That is, the predication of my decision of what to do on my ability to accept anyone else acting as I intend to do in such circumstances, has a prudential ground. My doing so, in other words, is itself a technique for the achievement of what I want. Playing the moral game can be justified by showing, in spite of appearances to the contrary, that it is really part of the technical game of want-satisfaction. Such a move gains plausibility by reminding us that we are social beings sharing certain desires with others, and therefore vulnerable to interference in the pursuit of our favoured goals, in the sense both that others may pursue what I want in conditions of scarcity, which means that all desires will not be satisfied, and that the routes to different goals may cross and lead to conflict between individuals. Morality becomes, therefore, a technique of mediation between conflicting desires, operating at either of these two levels. If we play morally, the message is, we shall more securely maximize our satisfactions. Such a view depends on an appeal to a hypothetical case where no one in fact plays morally and in which the individual can see that he would be worse off.

Yet, just because it does appeal to a hypothetical situation, this view provides no answer to the man who, intelligently, perceives that most people are not in fact going to stop playing morally, and argues that the wisest course, judged prudentially, is to capitalize on this. The fact that most people will go on being moved by moral considerations is, on the technical view, another relevant fact in the individual's pursuit of his ends, and one which he can turn to his advantage. Morality, just because it is a way of mediating conflicting desires, cannot be the final court of appeal for the individual in deciding what to do, and hence what is to his advantage. If moral considerations are important to me because of the advantage they bring, there will be cases where I can turn other people's morality to my advantage and win the game. And such a conclusion is difficult to avoid if morality is a guide to action in the same way as any other set of technical considerations. It also shows why the moral distinction between the morally arrogant and the considerate becomes impossible to draw, for in so far as they are both in the moral game for what they can get out of it, the only sort of relevant distinction is between those who play and win and those who play and lose. The arrogant man becomes at most someone who plays ineffectively; but this account would cope neither with the successful but haughty nor with those who hide their arrogance to further their own ends.

3. CONSEQUENCES OF THE ASSIMILATION

Earlier I listed certain consequences of the purposive paradigm for the sense which 'reason', 'change', 'development' and 'problem' could take in that context. Where morality is assimilated in the suggested way, that account will apply equally to 'moral reason', 'moral development' and 'moral problem'. A man has reason for doing something if to do it provides a passage to what he desires. Moral considerations can weigh with someone only if they too contribute to the achievement of his goals. I have, of course, simplified the suggested routes to assimilation. They have, in fact, resulted in two suggested methods. The one, as I have noted, reads morality as a further means to cope with the social nature of a man's pursuit of his goals. The other, concentrating on individual rather than social preconditions of purposive behaviour, sees morality as identifying certain fundamental requirements of the individual if he is to have any further goals. As such, the latter view sees morality as setting certain goals, such as freedom from injury, mental health, and so forth, which must be achieved if the general run of purposive action is to be possible. But even in this form, such goals are no different from those, such as freedom from other's interference, which are means to further ends. On either reading, morality is concerned with the means for successful goal achievement. Moral reasons, like any other within the purposive paradigm, take the form of facts which have weight with an individual because they indicate ways to the goals which determine his desires.

As such, moral development, like progress in any skill, is a process of the acquisition of new and better knowledge of the means towards certain goals. And because our pursuit of our purposes exists within an ever changing social environment, such development is often the adaptation to changed conditions. As Hare notes, a generation may find 'that conditions have changed (for example, through a protracted war or an industrial revolution) and that the principles in which they have been brought up are no longer adequate'. (*LM* p. 72) Given this fact, adequacy must be reattained and one's principles changed, else one's desires will go unsatisfied.

Problems do not arise for a man from his possession of moral notions; for the central problem, the satisfaction of wants, is prior logically to the operation of morality as technique. Moral problems are a species of technical problem, concerned largely with the determination of possible outcomes of one's acts and their effects on the achievement of one's aims. Moral problems have complexity, for they require an arithmetic complicated by the only vaguely calculable nature of what is assessed, the effects on one's desires, but not an importance for the individual different in kind from the normal run of practical difficulty. Moral mistakes are miscalculations or failures in preparation; remorse, in so far as it is not totally outside of rational appraisal, is a species of regret for lost opportunities.

4. TWO EXAMPLES

The tale told by this account is pretty adequate for the portrayal of certain kinds of moral case, and it will help bring out its inadequacy as a general account of morality to look at a couple of such examples. For what these help to emphasize is not that moral considerations cannot play the sort of role I have depicted, but that that role is itself open to obviously moral criticism. And that would be a rather strange fact if this were an adequate general account. Once the accusation of having ulterior motives for allowing moral considerations to play a role in one's actions is seen *as* an accusation and not a remark about the logic of moral discourse, the way will be clear to consider what account can emerge of actions which have moral, but not prudential, reasons.

Consider the following portrait:

Having always been the pet and pride of the household, waited on by mother, sisters, governess, and maids, as if she had been a princess in exile, she naturally found it difficult to think her own pleasure less important than others made it, and when it was positively thwarted, felt an astonished resentment. Gwendolen's nature was not remorseless, but she liked to make her penances easy, and now that she was twenty and more, some of her native force had turned into a self-control by which she guarded herself from penitential humiliation. There was more show of fire and will in her than ever, but there was more calculation underneath it.[3]

We have here a tolerable picture of moral development as comprehended by the technical account. Gwendolen

[3] George Eliot *Daniel Deronda* pp. 53–4. Penguin ed.

considers what she wants a priority in deciding what to do, although George Eliot intends this as a sad reflection on her character, rather than as a conceptual remark about the nature of human action. People can, however, impinge on the satisfaction of Gwendolen's desires by what they think of her and what they do because of this. To be well-liked is itself satisfying, and makes others malleable to one's interests. Good opinion can be sought and appearances kept up by undergoing penances, if light ones, in the approved style. (I am probably being too hard on Gwendolen. But at least it is possible for this to be too harsh a judgement, rather than a depiction of how things must be in a moral situation.) To avoid the irritation of the necessity of penances, she has become more calculating: she considers carefully the possible reactions of others to what she plans to do, and, where consonant with her own best interests, she tries to avoid giving displeasure. But just to put the matter like this indicates how far she is from allowing the standards in terms of which the displeasure is generated to play a part in her own actions. She will pay attention to those standards only if to do so will achieve more of what she wants than if she ignores them. Hence, she will dispense with them whenever seems most profitable.

Gwendolen's case, in other words, requires a *contrast* with those in which actions are performed for non-prudential reasons. This is particularly evident in her *semblance* of moral concern in order to avoid the moral disapproval of others.[4] Not only, therefore, does she calculate the effects of such disapproval on the achievement of her ends, but she utilizes the possibilities for gaining approval provided by the paradigmatic moral case through apparently acting for moral reasons. Such semblance, whilst parasitic on the real thing, is moti-

---

[4] Once again, I intrude no personal judgement here. It is for moral philosophy to articulate the distinction indicated in talk of 'semblance of moral concern', not ignore it.

vated by what would be, on the purposive account, the best
of designs.

> 'Gwendolen desires above all things to have a horse to ride
> —a pretty, light, lady's horse', said Mrs. Davilow . . . 'Do
> you think we can manage it?' . . . 'We could lend her the
> pony sometimes', said Mrs. Gascoigne . . . 'That might be
> inconveniencing others, aunt, and would be no pleasure to
> me. I cannot endure ponies', said Gwendolen, 'I would
> rather give up some other indulgences and have a horse.'
> (p. 65)

The effect produced by juxtaposing the refusal to take the
pony with the phrase 'That might be inconveniencing others'
depends on cases where the latter really would be the reason.
But Gwendolen spoils things by immediately indicating the
more important consideration, that it would be no pleasure
to her. Gwendolen uses such devices, however incompetently,
to avoid the censure which would follow a more blatant
assertion of her right to pleasure, a 'right' which, in turn, is
parasitic on a moral idea, for it is not equivalent merely to her
wanting certain things. The frustration of those desires is
accompanied by 'astonished resentment'. The present situation, where her family have just suffered a crippling reversal
in their financial affairs, needs careful handling if her ends are
to be achieved and censure avoided. It requires, therefore, the
semblance of moral concern. Far from epitomizing the
paradigmatic way in which moral notions can enter into a
man's actions, Gwendolen is portrayed as standing in a
certain kind of perverted relation to the moral considerations
which have a role in her life.

My second example illustrates another kind of role which
moral considerations can play. At the beginning of this
chapter, I noted two possible ways in which morality may be
assimilated to the purposive paradigm. The first, and by far

the most popular in Anglo-Saxon philosophy, is to identify it with a further kind of means to already existent goals. The second, no longer in vogue, is to see it as the origin of certain goals, logically similar to any other kind in purposive activity. Within this view, morality provides a picture of a certain kind of person to be. Such a conception suffers from one major difficulty at the start, for we can ask why it is that failure to pursue such goals is *blamed*, whereas other choices of goal are deemed a matter of personal taste. Such discrimination looks itself suspiciously like moral disapproval. Leaving this aside for the moment, let us consider a case which can be described as portraying a man 'seeking a moral goal' and ask whether this is a possible account of the way moral considerations must enter into a man's actions.

My example is taken from the early chapters of Conrad's novel *Lord Jim*. Jim is a young and promising ship's officer, and we are left in no doubt that he has a certain conception of 'the worthwhile life' described in moral terms. This enters in an important way into what he thinks and does. The picture of this life is derived from the 'light literature' of sea adventure, and portrays the life of the heroic naval officer. Jim finds little satisfaction in the prosaic life at sea, preferring rather 'thoughts . . . of valorous deeds: he loved those dreams and the sureness of imaginary achievements. They were the best parts of life, its secret truth, its hidden reality.' (p. 15)[5] Consonant with his conception of the heroic life as goal, he considers himself in constant preparation 'for all the difficulties that can beset one on land and water. He confessed proudly to this kind of foresight. He had been elaborating dangers and defences, expecting the worst, rehearsing the best . . .'. (p. 70)

Here we have a familiar group of words: the end in view (the achievement of the worthwhile life of heroic adventure), preparations towards its achievement, and the foresight

[5] Page references to the Everyman edition.

needed for this. If we look at these in a more familiar context we should get an account something like the following. A mountaineer may have as his goal the ascent of a particular mountain. In pursuit of his goal he makes certain preparations in the light of the various difficulties and dangers he foresees. He may make adequate preparation and yet still fail to achieve his goal. Such failure is not in itself blameworthy, blame attaching rather to the failure to take adequate precautions, to have done what could reasonably be expected in order to achieve the goal.

Jim's case, however, is rather different. His preparation consists in imagining dangers and his courage in facing them. Unlike thinking about the dangers of the climb and how to tackle them, this can be assessed as neither efficient nor inefficient, neither adequate nor inadequate. The idea of preparing correctly is that of reducing dangers to a minimum in the pursuit of some further goal. The dangers Jim faces, however, are the very vehicle for his heroism. The analogy, that is, lies not with the dangers in their relation to the mountaineer's preparations, but with the dangers in their relation to how the mountaineer will face them if they occur. And in respect of this, the mountaineer is in the same position as Jim. Preparation is connected with foreseeing what *may* occur in the pursuit of one's goals. But the dangers Jim foresees are not obstacles to the achievement of a goal which, if overcome, is made more accessible, since in his case to overcome is to succeed, although not in the sense of overcoming the effects of the obstacles on the pursuit of some further goal, but of overcoming their effects on *him*. 'Foresight' in Jim's case is not a matter of judging what may occur, but of determining not to be afraid. 'I know I shall be brave' is not a prediction as 'I know there will be avalanches' is. Whereas for the mountaineer, to blame himself for lack of success is to blame his failure in preparation, it is Jim's failure to act courageously which he sees as blameworthy.

If these are differences in the consequences of failing to achieve the goal, further differences appear if we look at the idea of successfully attaining it. If I want to be, say, a good engineer and I succeed, what counts as my success is determined by the standards of engineering which I share with my fellow engineers. If I say 'I am a good engineer', and they agree, we both appeal to the same grounds to justify our statements. They may, of course, disapprove of me for saying so and call it boasting, but that will not affect their judgement that I am what I say I am. Their disapproval has different and non-conflicting grounds from their judgement of my worth as an engineer. But if the term denoting the condition achieved is a moral one, the situation is altered, for the statement that a man has achieved this, made by others, is itself a piece of moral approval. There is no room here for the distinction between the approval expressed by 'He's a good engineer' and the disapproval of a man for his saying so of himself.

In the engineering case, the first and third person judgements both appealed to the same grounds, the standards of engineering. Let us consider for a moment the parallel judgements in Jim's case: 'I am a hero' on the one hand, and 'He is a hero' on the other. If a man rescues a wounded soldier in the face of enemy fire and we are asked why we say he is heroic, we should point to the mortal danger of his act and the fact that he 'could' have left the man to his fate. In this way we mark certain 'alternatives' to what in fact the man did. But this by no means implies that the man himself was faced by a choice between alternatives. If it did, then our judgement that the man was a hero would depend on the fact that he chose to rescue the soldier rather than performing one of the alternatives and would, therefore, be defeasible if the man denied there was a choice. However, the fact that a man may, when asked for an account, reply 'I couldn't leave him there' does not lead us to withdraw our judgement, but, on the contrary, reinforces it. Thus, within such a moral context the two statements 'He could have done otherwise' and 'I couldn't do otherwise' are compatible.

Now, if the grounds for the first-person judgement 'I am a hero' are to be the same as those of the third person judgement we have just examined, one of them must be 'I could have done otherwise'. This locution is indistinguishable, where it does not indicate the acceptance of blame, from 'I could have chosen differently'. Since this implies the presence of some common criterion for judging between the alternatives faced, the act would not be performed simply because the soldier could not rescue himself. Yet it is the presence of precisely such a reason that often weighs with an observer in judging the rescuer to be heroic. In such cases, the first and third person statements cannot be made on the same grounds. Furthermore, whereas the third but not the first-person statement is one of moral approval, the latter leaves the speaker open to the moral criticism of boasting. It may be a mistake not to realize one's worth as an engineer. But is it a mistake not to realize one's moral worth?

It seems, therefore, that the assimilation of at least some moral considerations to the roles of means or ends leads to an inability to account for moral distinctions we do in fact make. If moral considerations are treated as means, it becomes a problem to depict Gwendolen's case as parasitic on others which embody a fundamentally different role for moral notions. If they are treated as goals, there seems no way of accounting for their peculiar importance, nor for the fact that claims to have attained them leave the speaker open to *moral* criticism. The further difficulties with the notions of 'moral change' and 'moral problem' bequeathed to ethics by the purposive paradigm will be treated in what follows.

2. Morality, Goals and Meaning

In the first chapter I tried to outline, and object to, the assimilation of the role moral considerations play in men's thoughts and actions to that provided within the purposive paradigm for means and goals. I shall have more to say about this in the chapter which follows this, where I shall look at the characteristic way in which moral and purposive notions enter into a man's relation with his past. But there is another possibility which I mentioned, but did not develop because it has played little part in the moral philosophies considered, namely, that moral notions might display some similarities with those associated with the relation of a man to the goals he pursues, a relation often indicated by saying 'Xing means a lot to him' or 'Xing is his whole life'. Given the difficulties about the assimilation of moral notions to goals, the implications of such similarities may well be strictly limited. However, I think they are interesting, and can help indicate things which are often ignored in discussions of purposive action as well as illuminating by comparison and contrast possible roles for moral notions.

1. WANTING AND REASONS

We must distinguish between those elements present in 'A giving reasons to B for doing x' and those in 'A having reasons for doing x'. We should in particular notice the differences between the roles played by statements of fact, intention, wanting and decision in each.

If A is asked by B why he is doing x, he may reply 'Xing is a way to y, y is a means to z and I want z'. 'Xing leads to y' and 'y is a means to z' are statements that may be true or false, and so A may be right or wrong about them. But whereas 'A wants z' is a similar case, 'I want z' is not. Wondering whether A wants z is wondering whether, for example, A would be pleased if I gave him z, or if he'll go for z rather than c if the opportunity arises, and so on. Wondering whether I want z is wondering whether to choose z rather than c, or wondering whether to pursue z at all. In other words, wondering whether I want z is trying to make a decision about what to do or to try to do, whereas wondering whether you want z is not. Although I can give you reasons why I am doing something by stating certain facts and saying 'I want x', and although you can give someone else reasons why I am doing something by stating certain facts and saying 'He wants x', 'I want x' is not a reason *I have* for doing it. 'I want x' is logically closer to statements for which I have reasons, like 'I'll do x' or 'I choose x', than to the statements of reasons themselves.

Within descriptions of what others are doing, 'He wants y' indicates the goal he pursues. To say 'He's doing x because he wants y' is much the same as saying 'He's doing x to get y'. To identify a man's wants is usually to identify the goals he pursues. In so far as goals provide reasons for action, they constitute the last link in the chain 'doing x because y, wanting y because z'. The statement 'I want z', within this context, specifies a goal. But such a phrase also occurs outside of goal-directed behaviour precisely to mark the absence of purpose. For example, a man who knows nothing of painting may be left waiting in a room with a canvas and some paints and brushes. He may put a dab of yellow on the canvas, and when asked why he did this, may reply 'I just wanted to'. Here it is equivalent to 'I just felt like it', and far from indicating whatever provides reasons for action, it indicates that the action had no reason in the purposive sense at all. Such a response eliminates the possibility of further discussion of reasons. Hence it must be distinguished from the 'I want to' which can indicate a goal, and where, as we have noted, although further reasons in terms of facts about means to the goal cannot be given for its pursuit, 'reason-giving' and the having of reasons are by no means ruled out.

2. REASONS AND GOALS

We can note two ways in which the idea of a goal can enter into a man's actions. Most obviously it enters in the provision of reasons for actions, providing the end to which certain things are means. Less obviously, it enters through the relation the man himself has to the goal. By this phrase I mean to include at least two kinds of related phenomena. First, that people can be asked, and very often say a great deal, about 'what they see in' the goals they pursue. Answers to this may be said to give their 'reasons', but these do not specify means to an end. Secondly, that when people give reasons for doing a particular act they very often indicate the importance which an activity or goal has for them and which provides a *non-instrumental* importance to the particular act itself.

As an example of the latter, consider the following conversation:

Q: Why are you going out?
A: To hear X; he's giving a talk tonight.
Q: Why go to listen to him?
A: Well, he's a grand old man of the discipline. I think I ought to go and hear him.

Now, that 'he is a grand old man of the discipline' is A's

reason for going, but it specifies neither a goal nor a means to one. It need not be that A thinks he will become a better anthropologist, or whatever, or learn something new by going. And this kind of reason-giving by an individual parallels explanations by others of why he is doing what he does in terms, not of the goals he pursues, but of the relation he has to the goal or activity: 'He cares a great deal about it, so he'll be there', 'He has a great respect for the man as an anthropologist', and so on. And these notions are clearly at least part of what we mean when we speak of the 'meaning' of the activity or goal for the person concerned. I shall return to this later in this chapter.

Such reason-giving as this is associated with the idea of giving reasons for one's pursuit of an activity or goal, for both can be said to indicate the nature of the importance of that activity or goal for the individual. It is characteristic of 'saying why' one pursues an activity or goal that such reason-giving takes the form of a description. Consider the following two examples.

> We would say then that the sociologist . . . is a person intensively, endlessly, shamelessly interested in the doings of men . . . He investigates communities, institutions and activities that one can read about everyday in the news-papers. Yet there is another excitement of discovery beckoning in his investigations. It is not the excitement of coming upon the totally unfamiliar, but rather the excitement of finding the familiar transformed in its meaning. The fascination of sociology lies in the fact that its perspective makes us see in a new light the very world in which we have lived all our lives.
>
> (P. Berger *Invitation to Sociology* pp. 30–3)

> The best mathematics is *serious* as well as beautiful— 'important' if you like, but the word is very ambiguous . . .

I am not thinking of the 'practical' consequences of mathematics . . . very little of mathematics is useful practically, and . . . that little is comparatively dull. The 'seriousness' of a mathematical theorem lies, not in its practical consequences, which are usually negligible, but in the *significance* of the mathematical ideas which it contains.

(G. Hardy *A Mathematician's Apology* p. 29)

Such descriptions do not indicate the consequences of the activity for any other; they are not concerned with 'practical consequences'. They involve the application of a range of terms like 'excitement', 'seeing in a new light', 'beauty', 'seriousness' and 'importance' in a particular context—being able to apply these in other contexts will not help one understand what is said here. Being *able to apply them* to mathematics or sociology is, in fact, part and parcel of coming to see something in these activities oneself and finding them important.

Georges Sorel, writing of the artists of the great Gothic cathedrals, provides an example which helps bring out more clearly the connection which can exist between a purposive activity and an agent which we mark when we speak of 'what a man sees in' an activity.

Among the stone carvers who sculptured the statues in the cathedral there were men of great talent who seemed always to have remained anonymous; nevertheless they produced masterpieces . . . We might question whether their contemporaries suspected that these artists of genius had raised edifices of imperishable glory; it seems very probable to me that the cathedrals were only admired by the artists.

(Sorel *Reflections on Violence* p. 246)[1]

[1] Trans. T. E. Hulme, ed. E. A. Shils, Collier, 1969.

C

We can look at these statues from at least two points of view: their importance for art, and their importance for their carvers. The 'imperishable glory' Sorel speaks of is to be understood through the terms of the art of sculpture: these artists set standards of carving and design in their work through which others could be introduced to what is excellent in art. The statues, understood as works of art divorced from their artists, are objects of artistic admiration, and can, therefore, play a role in other people's lives. Looked at from the other perspective, however, we may ask, not what these statues meant for art, but what they meant for the artists concerned. Sorel speaks of the relation of the artists to their work in terms of a 'striving towards perfection which manifests itself, in spite of the absence of any personal, immediate, and proportional reward'. (p. 246) In emphasizing this absence, Sorel is warning us not to look outside art for the terms in which we understand the relation of the artists to their work. The 'perfection' which provides their importance to their carvers is artistic, and it is this which provides the point for them of their labours. The importance of a particular work to its creator shows in the 'striving' towards an artistic perfection, understood through notions of beauty, form, texture, and so on, which have their home in art. It would appear both in the efforts the man put into his work, and in the way he talks about the problems he is faced with and the sort of solutions he is considering. In other words, it will appear in the absorption of the man in his work.

The reasons which the man has for what he does as a sculptor are drawn from the problems of his art: they will not make reference to external considerations. They will take the form of facts about the sculpture (for example, 'that the proportions of the head aren't right yet'), which involve the application of artistic terms and which are reasons for the man because he has a certain artistic goal. But the man's 'care' and 'respect' for his art are not further reasons he has for what he does; they are not additional facts which weigh with him in determining what he does. They can, however, enter into observers' explanations of his actions and there they indicate the man's relation to his work by emphasizing that he has solely artistic reasons for what he does. They relate, that is, not to the reasons the man has, but to the fact that they are the only reasons he has: and that, of course, is not a reason the man can have himself. The importance of an activity to a man, in this sense, comes out, not in the fact that he has reasons for his actions which refer to anything beyond the activity, even to his personal situation, but in the absence of such reasons. I shall relate this in a moment to the idea of 'making sense' of one's life.

Having reasons for pursuing an activity, where this does not involve reference to external goals, is being able to give oneself to it: that is, to act solely for reasons intelligible within the activity. Giving reasons for one's involvement in it will be describing the activity in a particular way, which description will involve, as we have seen, the ability to apply certain terms to what one does.

It is against this background that we can understand the other sort of case I mentioned at the beginning of this section, the having of reasons and the use of 'ought' where what is done, although conceived within a purposive activity, has a non-instrumental importance for the agent. The act is not done because of what it will bring towards the achievement of a goal, but because, given that the goal plays the role it does in the man's life, the act has a non-instrumental importance, indicated by the use of 'ought' or 'must'. And here the 'because' points not to the provision of means to an end, but to the relation the man himself has to the goal. For the observer, it is a way in which the care and respect the man has for the goal or activity shows itself, but that care or respect is, again, not a reason the man has for what he does. I shall discuss this further in section 4 below. I want to turn now to a case, not of the non-instrumental importance of an action for an individual, expressed by his remark 'I ought to do this' or 'I must do this', conceived within a purposive activity, but of moral importance and to relate both of these to the kind of 'importance' which an act can have for a man.

3. MORAL IMPORTANCE AND MEANING

To speak of what is important to a man is, in contexts like these, to speak of what a man finds significance in. It would be possible to stress, for example, the relation Sorel's artists had to their art by saying that for them 'their life was their art'. By this we should indicate, of course, the care and attention they paid to their work, but we should also be pointing to something else indicated by speaking of 'their life'. Knowing that one is going to die is a feature of any life, but the way the importance of this fact appears for people differs a great deal. Where we can say that for someone an activity 'is' his life, we are indicating a relation of the self to an activity within which the importance of death can appear in a particular way. For example, one of Sorel's artists may think of his death in terms of his inability to finish a particular work, or in terms of what he has achieved. In such contexts, thought about one's death is an occasion for thinking about one's work. In the first case, the regret that his death is near *is* the regret that his work will go unfinished, just as if in the second he had said 'It has been a good life' his thankfulness is for what he has been able to do as an artist. In both cases, the importance, or lack of it, of the man's death is seen in terms of the man's involvement with his work. Such cases are to be contrasted with ones where the prospect of death judges one's engagement in an activity. Take a similar case. Realizing for example, that one's blindness is due to the reading and writing required by an activity, a man may curse the day he began with it, or he may not. In neither case would the consequences of blindness be minimized, but the importance of them is different for each. In one, we might say, the blindness is used to judge the man's participation in the activity, in the other that participation provides a way of regarding the blindness. And a similar contrast exists between cases where one's death can be comprehended from within one's involvement with an activity, and ones where it cannot. A certain class of these cases consists of those in which a man faces death because of his involvement, whether through, for example, persecution or overwork, and here we shall find a similar distinction. I shall consider this sort of example in relation to a case of a man facing death for a moral reason.

It is a characteristic difficulty of the purposive view of morality to make sense of moral actions involving the sacrifice of a man's life. The reason for this is fairly clear. If behaving according to certain moral injunctions promotes certain things that I want, then I have a reason for so behaving in as far as they in fact contribute to my success. For any moral act I have a reason for doing it just so far as it promotes the ends I have in view. But faced with the certainty of death, such reasons necessarily become inoperative, for death is the end of any short or long term gain for me. Given my reasons for acting morally, I have none for a moral act which I know will result in my death. And yet, difficult as it may be to characterize such acts, they are conceivable, and not merely in moral contexts. Purposive activities, as we have seen, similarly provide a context within which men can make sense of their deaths.

I shall first consider an intermediate case, which indicates, I think, the kind of account we should give of the moral example, and which can illuminate the idea of 'having a moral reason'. A has been a friend of B for some time, and one night whilst staying with him, he hears a noise. Going out to investigate, he surprises a burglar and is shot in the leg.

The leg is severely damaged and will leave A lame. One can think of two different sorts of relation A may have to the fact that he is lame, which seem diametrically opposed. In the first, A responds by thinking 'If only I'd never known B', and curses his ill-fortune in being in the house on that particular night. In the other, the lameness is not the occasion for regretting the relationship with B; perhaps he thinks of the injury as an unfortunate thing which may happen to anyone.[2] Now, what is not being denied in this latter case is the seriousness of the injury, in one sense: in both cases A understands that he will never walk properly again and that this will seriously affect the pursuit of his various activities. It is not as if the absence of the thought 'I wish I'd never known B' marks a misunderstanding or minimizing of the consequences. The seriousness of the injury understood in terms of these effects on A's activities is the same for both. But in another sense of 'seriousness' this is not so: that sense, namely, in which the seriousness is brought out by the expression 'I wish I'd never known B' or its absence. Neither of these would be possible if the injury were not regarded as serious in the other sense. Bringing out the differences between the two cases is bringing out the absence in one of a way of thinking which encompasses the effects of the injury within the terms provided by A's relationship with B. In the second case, the seriousness of the injury, understood in terms of its effects, is regarded from within the relationship. The relationship, we might say, assesses the injury: it provides a way of regarding it.

I want now to elaborate some of the notions contained in this account by considering a case in which a man has a moral reason for going to his death: once more, I refer to Conrad's novel *Lord Jim*. In the last part of the novel, Jim is settled in a native village to which he has brought a time of peace, the

[2] I owe to Tony Palmer (Southampton University) this emendation to an earlier draft.

first it has known for many years. This peace is disturbed by the entrance of a marauder, Gentleman Brown, and his gang, searching for food and plunder. Jim being absent at the time, the villagers defend themselves against Brown, and could have destroyed him and his gang completely, but for Dain Waris, the headman's son, who persuades them to wait for Jim's verdict. Jim returns, and after a conversation with Brown, tells the natives to let the gang go free.

> He was ready to answer with his life for any harm that should come to them if the white men with beards were allowed to retire. (p. 289)

Brown, determined to avenge himself on the village that had thwarted him, massacres a party of villagers, including Dain Waris, on his way to the coast. Jim, hearing what has happened, goes to the headman in the full knowledge of what will ensue, and is shot dead. The question of why Jim knowingly went to his death is clearly intelligible, as, therefore, is the associated notion of Jim's 'reasons' for this action.

Let us approach the relation which exists for Jim between the fact of the massacre and the prospect of his own death, by looking at what he says when urged to act in alternative ways. We must once again be careful with this term: it is we, and the other observers of his action, who see these other courses of action as 'alternatives', as 'other things he could do'. It by no means follows that they were alternatives for him. I shall elaborate on this in a moment. Tamb' Itam, his servant, tells Jim they must fight for their lives, but Jim refuses to consider the idea: 'I have no life'. (p. 302) His wife tries to persuade him to fight and to flee the country:

> She cried 'fight' into his ear. She could not understand. There was nothing to fight for . . . 'Will you fight?' she cried. 'There is nothing to fight for', he said, 'nothing is

lost' . . . 'Will you fly?' she cried again. 'There is no
escape', he said . . . 'Do you remember the night I prayed
you to leave me, and you said it was impossible . . .'
'Enough, poor girl', he said, 'I should not be worth having'.
(pp. 302–4)

This is the sort of situation in which we should say that Jim
felt he *had* to do what he did. His remark, that he 'would not
be worth having' else, points to the fact that the importance
of the act is, in some sense, bound up with Jim's conception
of himself. However, this phrase is difficult, for its use can
easily lead to a conflation between cases where, in indicating
an act's importance for himself, a man says 'I couldn't live
with myself if I didn't do this', with others of self-aggrandize-
ment, where we speak of a man having a sense of his own
importance. Our present difficulty is to see in what sense
Jim's self is involved in the act we have described. I think we
can do this by looking at the nature of the 'necessity' we
indicate when we say 'Jim had to do this', which points to the
importance he sees in the act. This sense of 'necessity' is,
therefore, bound up with the notion of 'importance' we are
considering.

Let us first of all ask whether Jim can be said to face
alternative courses of action in this situation. Jim's remark
'I should not be worth having' is said in response to sug-
gestions of alternative courses of action. Can it be said to
constitute a reason for opting for the course he took rather
than the others suggested? Usually when we speak of the
reasons someone has for not pursuing one line of conduct and
engaging in another, we are trying to understand the reasons
behind a *choice*. Characteristically, such a choice operates by
deciding for certain consequences and not others, and this is
possible because in doing x a man brings about p, whereas in
not doing x he brings about not-p. The choice to do x depends
on the possibility of assessing the consequences, p and not-p,

in terms of some standard, for the advantage of p must be contrasted with the disadvantage of not-p. Such a standard will show how it is that the fact that xing leads to p counts as a reason for doing x, and therefore for not doing not-x. Now, it seems that the reasons Jim gives are not of this kind. He does not provide an account of how going to Doramin will procure or promote some goal he seeks. But, of course, the purposive model provides other approaches. When I am asked why I pursue the goals I do, some at least of these will not be things that I want because of their production of something further. Where the instrumental reason-giving stops, I can have no further instrumental reasons. Since the sense which 'choice', 'alternative' and 'decision' had in the instrumental context depended on the fact that the pursuit of a goal provided the standard in terms of which something could count *as* a choice, alternative, or decision, if in showing why one pursues certain goals, instrumental reasons are absent, there will be no place there for speaking of 'choice', 'alternative' or 'decision', at least in the same sense. (Thus, to say one 'chooses' here may simply indicate that one is not being coerced or has any other kind of ulterior reason.) That is, there will be nothing further which could provide the grounds for choice, alternatives or decision, and, in instrumental terms, I have no reason for pursuing such goals. To provide reasons here is, as we have seen, a way of expressing one's dedication to the goal or activity. These two senses of reason provide for at least three interpretations which 'I must do x' can bear within the purposive model.

In the first, 'I must do x' has reasons in the normal instrumental sense, but is used to stress the superiority of xing over any possible rival. For example, in the face of a certain situation on the stock-market and in the light of my desire for wealth, I may say 'I must buy S shares', thereby indicating that in terms of potential profit S shares are superior at the present time to any others. In the second, 'I must do this', or more usually, 'I have to do this', indicates the importance, not of a means, but of a goal to oneself. In dismissing the idea of ulterior motives, a man may say, for example, 'Archaeology is just something I have to do; I wouldn't be living if I gave it up.' Here, 'I must' marks the way in which one's life is bound up with the activity. In the third, we find, as I have noted above, a similar use to this, but where a particular act rather than an activity is the subject of the 'I must'. 'I must go to listen to X' is of this kind in cases where there are no instrumental reasons for the act.

Jim's case does not conform to the first of these models. Apart from those considerations we noted in the first chapter, although connected with them, two features of a more mundane example can show this. Consider this brief dialogue. 'I felt I had to help that old lady across the road.' 'Why?' 'Well, she was old and infirm and couldn't get over by herself.' We recognize this as a moral case because it falls under a moral concept 'charity'. Does charity enter into the action in the way a goal would? Firstly, 'charity' enters primarily in observers' accounts of what is done. In the first person there is a possible moral distinction between someone who says 'I did it out of charity' and someone who merely says 'She was old and infirm.' Cases like the former are often identified by observers not as cases of charity, but rather, for example, of patronizing behaviour. They are felt to be 'in the wrong spirit', even though, in one sense the end result is the same, the old woman getting over the road. Moral appraisal does not stop, that is, at such 'external' results. In the case of goal-directed behaviour, both the observer's description and the reason-giving of the individual will specify the goal in question.

The second thing we can note is the role of the idea of 'indifference' in purposive behaviour. Where we have a goal, it provides a standard for choosing between courses of action in terms of the contribution made by the act to the goal's achievement. Where two courses are seen as making a potentially equal contribution, there could be no instrumental reason for choosing one rather than the other. Which I do, so long as one is done, is a matter of indifference. Hence, it is intelligible to say here 'As far as the pursuit of the goal is concerned, doing x or doing y is a matter of indifference to me'. But if someone were to say 'As far as charity goes, doing x or doing y is a matter of indifference to me', it could be morally objected that the man was not concerned with charity at all. Moral cases where we find such a decision must be made are the stuff, not of indifference, but of moral 'dilemmas', and the use of such a term marks the fact that there is room here for caring about one's inability to perform one of the actions.

Our second model too, is unhelpful. The reason-giving for a goal, where it is non-instrumental, is not itself the provision of reasons for any individual act, being rather the expression of what the agent sees as of value in his activity. The moral reason, however, explains the performance of a particular act. There is, however, a certain similarity between the moral case and our third possiblity, the non-instrumental act performed within a purposive activity. Thus, just as 'This is a case of charity' does not enter as a reason the man has for helping the old lady, so 'This is a case of caring about one's subject' does not enter as a reason the anthropologist has for going to listen to his speaker, even though an observer may explain the actions in terms of charity and dedication. Again, the regret that he could not attend two simultaneous talks need not be explicable in terms of the anthropologist's lost opportunities to further his knowledge. It is possible here too to care about one's inability to do two things, in a way not explicable in terms of the goal or pursuit of the activity itself. For all that, however, the moral notions do not presuppose the ideas of goals in the way those notions that relate to a man's relation to a goal obviously do. Hence, the 'I must' that stems from such a relation cannot be identified with the 'I must' of the moral case.

These considerations allow us to say the following about Jim's 'I must do this'. The act matters to Jim neither as means, nor goal, nor in terms of his relation to a goal, nor even under the rubric 'This is morally good.' And this, in a way, is all we can say, apart from locating the moral area within which the act was performed. I mean by this that not going to the head-man would have been a betrayal of a relationship which, like the friendship we considered above, is indicated by moral categories. (I shall try to articulate the way these categories enter into action in section 4 below.)

Jim's remark 'I must do this' was made in the full know-ledge that he was going to his death. The relationship within which the act was performed was, then, one which, in the sense I spoke of above, provided for Jim a way of making sense of his death. This is an important point, for the relation-ship must, in a fairly straightforward sense, be *terminated* by the act. We could not, therefore, confuse Jim's 'I must do this' with cases where people say 'I must do this to keep our friendship/marriage going'. Such remarks as these are only intelligible when there is already something wrong with the relationship, and the important thing in Jim's case is that this would only be so if he had failed to do what he saw as neces-sary. Only if he had not gone to the headman would there have been betrayal of the relationship, and hence there could only have been something wrong with the relationship if he had failed to go to his death. And this is apt to sound para-doxical, for Jim's death terminates the relationship. How can a man have a reason for dying conceived solely within the relationship he has with others when his death brings that relationship to an end? However, this is not the sense of 'end' that accompanies the idea of people drifting apart, no longer feeling bound together, but rather indicates the obvious point that Jim's death marks the end of his actions understood in any way whatever. Hence, what seems problematic is how it is possible for a man to have a reason for dying in any sense; and this, as I have noted, is a problem only if 'reason' here is read as 'instrumental reason'. In Jim's case, this problem centres on his remark 'I should be worth nothing if I did not do it', for this could be read as if Jim hoped to gain something by what he does. Is 'I should be worth nothing' equivalent to 'I shall be worth (something/a great deal) if I do it'? And this is clearly connected with the question of whether moral failure, of the kind hinted at in Jim's remark, is the opposite of moral success. Jim's remark could only be the equivalent of 'I should be worth something' if 'I should be worth nothing' has a future reference: if 'should' is equivalent to 'will be'. If it were, then, of course, Jim's action becomes unintelligible, for what he does leads to his death and the end of any possible advantage for him.[3] But not only does Jim not decide to do what he does in terms of the consequences of his act, but a moral judgement that he acted well would not be predicated on these consequences either. The 'worth' Jim speaks of has no reference to consequences nor to any sense of his own 'value' after the event. What then does he speak of? The answer to this can, I think, only be one thing: the act itself. What is being said is something about the act of dying from within the context of the relationship which called it forth. The death does not assess the relationship, which would indeed have made Jim's act unintelligible, but, rather, the relationship assesses the death. In this way we have a parallel

[3] There is another kind of case, however. A may may die in order to achieve fame, or become a martyr (cf. the possibilities envisaged by T. S. Eliot in his play *Murder in the Cathedral*). In so far as this is being motivated by a desire for the good opinion of others, it presupposes the terms used in this hoped for praise. The questions then become (i) whether this praise would be forthcoming if the motivation were known (whether a moral distinction would be drawn by those others involved as observers); and (ii) whether any act so praised must be done for such a reason. It is these questions I consider here.

to the cases of injury considered above. As we saw there, no misunderstanding of the nature of what happens, one's death or injury, is implied. Death is understood as the end of one's activities, and is seen as the inevitable outcome of what one is doing. (The question of the risk involved does not arise, in the way it would if some advantage were sought.) Given such a summary of what death is for an individual, its seriousness for him, the way this seriousness appears to him, can differ. Seeing that he is going to die, a man may curse his luck at getting into a lethal situation and determine if at all possible to get out. Death as the end of the individual's actions is seen here as something to be struggled against: its importance is contained in its consequences for the pursuit of his aims. Given such a perspective, the move we find in Jim's case from 'I would be killed' to 'I must go to the headman' would become unintelligible. The question, therefore, is how we understand such a move.

4. MORALITY AND INFERENCE

When we speak of inference we speak of conclusions drawn from the fact that certain things are the case: a statement of the 'conclusion' is drawn from a statement of certain facts as 'premises'. The problem of moral inference is to understand the sort of conclusion Jim draws, 'I must go' and the performance of this action, from certain facts 'That the villagers have been massacred', or in more mundane examples, one's helping the old lady over the road from the fact that she is old and standing uncertainly by the roadside. In such cases as these the conclusion is drawn in words and, or, actions: Jim sees what has happened and goes, one sees the old lady and helps her. Such cases present examples of the connection between statements or perceptions of facts which provide reasons and the action done for those reasons, a problem we find equally within the purposive paradigm and which is there usually tackled under the heading of 'practical inference'.

The impetus for such questions, and, in the case of practical reasoning, the model provided for their answer, has come from the treatment of theoretical inference, the drawing of a statement as conclusion from other statements as grounds. Such a beginning is useful, for it emphasizes the distinction between the premises and conclusion on the one hand, and the form of the inference on the other. If we take as an example one sort of derivation of statements which has usually been taken as paradigmatic, we can see what this amounts to. Taking a 'deductive' inference, we can show that it is coherent to move from 'Socrates is a man' to 'Socrates is mortal' by producing another statement 'All men are mortal', because with the additional statement we can display 'Socrates is mortal' as a 'conclusion' of a deductive inference. I can, therefore, give *reasons* for saying 'Socrates is mortal' by saying 'All men are mortal and Socrates is a man.' But we cannot give *reasons* in this way for saying that 'Socrates is mortal' does indeed follow from those premises. If we try we get into a well known regress. I justify my conclusion of 'Socrates is mortal' from the premise 'Socrates is a man' by producing the statement 'All men are mortal.' But I don't justify this justification through another premise 'If all men are mortal and Socrates is a man, then Socrates is mortal.' If I did this, I should need some yet further premise to justify this derivation, and so on. At some point, the reasons given are all that can be given, and the conclusion is drawn without more ado: justification comes to an end. That 'end' in this case is the setting out of the 'reasons' and 'conclusion' in the form of a deductive inference. There can be no justification for this form of connection, of inference, comparable with the justification for conclusions drawn within it by the presentation of reasons. In this way, the form of connection does not enter into the inference, the particular case of connection, *as a further reason.* If we are asked why 'Socrates is mortal' follows from 'All men are mortal and Socrates is a man' we can do no more than show it conforms to other cases of what we call 'deductive argument'. We can do this by producing other examples or setting out the form of the examples in a symbolism, but both of these are procedures as 'questionable' as the original case.

The distinction, therefore, between particular cases of premises and conclusions and the form of connection is that between particular statements and *what makes them count as* 'premises' and 'conclusions'. As such, the form of connection can be itself neither premise nor conclusion. So, whenever we have a case of inference, we can usefully ask both what are counted here as premises and conclusion, and what makes them count as 'premises' and 'conclusion'. Let us, then, turn to cases of 'practical reasoning', which are usually taken from the purposive paradigm. Consider the connection expressed by 'so' in the following: 'If the excavation is to be carried out, forty men will be needed; so, I'll employ them.' 'So I'll employ them' is an expression of intention; as such, it can be said neither to be true nor false. Yet the 'so' indicates that it in some sense 'follows from' a statement which is straightforwardly true or false: 'if the excavation is to be carried out, forty men will be needed'. But not only is 'so I'll employ them' neither true nor false, it isn't even a conclusion which anyone must draw from the premises. Anyone can agree with the calculation that forty men will be needed to carry the excavation out, but only certain people will draw the conclusion 'so I'll employ them'. On both counts, such a case of practical inference differs from the theoretical paradigm, for there the conclusion is itself true or false, else it could not be derived from the premises, and who draws the conclusion is considered irrelevant. To say the conclusion follows or not we do not have to refer to the person presenting the argument.

In the theoretical case, whether the conclusion did follow

or not depended on the form of connection within which the particular statements count as 'premises' and 'conclusion'. A faulty inference is one that purports to satisfy the form but doesn't; if it doesn't set out to satisfy it, it cannot be judged faulty by that form, just as an inference like 'Leeds have beaten Cardiff twice this season, so they'll win on Saturday' is not a faulty deductive inference. We said, too, that the form of inference did not enter into particular inferences as either premises or conclusion, but as what makes those particular statements count as 'premises' and 'conclusion'. But the case of practical inference presents a problem, for *who* is drawing the inference is obviously central: from certain facts some people draw certain conclusions in expressions of intention and in action, while others do not without leaving themselves open to a charge of 'inconsistency'. Agents, that is, seem to operate as themselves forms of connection, in some sense.

If the same facts can be present to two people and yet they draw different conclusions in intention and action, to ask what we can say about their differences will illuminate the sense in which agents are 'forms of connection'. The obvious candidate here within the purposive paradigm is the pursuit of goals. What differs between A and B when, given that they both know that p, A does x whereas B does not, is that A, but not B, sees that to some goal he pursues it is relevant that p and that by doing x because p that goal can be pursued here. The model of the agent as form of connection suggested here is this. 'That p' constitutes the reason for the intention or action, the premises for the conclusion. What makes that a 'premise' and a 'conclusion', but does not enter into the inference as either, is A's pursuit of the goal. This, however, tells only half the story. That 'that p' is an *intelligible* reason for doing x is provided, not by A's pursuit of the goal, but by the goal itself. That excavating here is a means of discovering if there was a Bronze Age settlement on this spot, and that

D

discovering this is a way of answering certain archaeological problems, is provided by the nature of archaeology, which is an activity many individuals may pursue. But that p is, not merely an intelligible reason for doing x, but the reason A has for doing x, is provided by A's pursuit of archaeology. We have, then, two separate 'forms of connection' on our hands within an example of practical reasoning. Firstly, there is the goal or activity which makes that p an intelligible reason for doing x; secondly, there is the agent's pursuit of the goal which makes that p a possible reason for him to do x. And neither of these enter as premises into the 'practical inference' he is engaged upon.

Now, moral inferences look closer to 'practical' than to 'theoretical' ones. The conclusions are often statements of intention and actions, or refusals to contemplate certain actions, and so on. Yet if they are not examples of goal directed behaviour, what will take the place of the goal and the agent's pursuit of it as the 'forms of connection' within which an intention is formulated or an action done? The answer in outline is, I think, something like this. What provides the intelligibility of a connection between certain facts and certain actions are moral concepts in terms of which doing something, described non-morally, can be seen as a case of an action described morally. Thus, seeing someone in financial difficulties and giving him money can be seen as an act of friendship. But the presence of two sets of terms, 'means' and 'goals', in the purposive case complicates any straightforward comparison or contrast. Unlike the goal-oriented case, in which the recognition of a certain act as a means to the goal in question is a necessary precondition of performing the associated act for that reason, it is by no means the case that the act must be seen by the agent *as* an act of friendship before he could be said to have a reason to do it. For there is a distinction between someone who does such an act within, as it were, a relationship of friendship, and one who does it because, for example, to do so will get others to call him 'a friend', even though the result, the gift or loan of the money, is the same in both cases. And this points to the second 'form of connection', what makes these facts a reason for the agent for doing a certain act, the place that certain moral notions have in his life. In the case of the man who does a certain act because it will be called an act of friendship, that fact becomes a further reason in his inference: as such the notion of friendship, through its application to the particular case, becomes part of the inference, which then requires a further factor, such as a goal, as a form of connection. Where 'This is an act of friendship' is a premise in the reasoning, that reasoning does not take its form of intelligibility from the role of the notion of friendship in the man's actions, whereas 'This is a means to the goal' must be present as a premise for a practical inference. In this respect, the notion of friendship is more like that of the goal or activity itself, for 'This is a piece of archaeology' does not enter as a premise in the archaeologist's reasoning, it is not an additional fact he must take into account. It rather would locate for an observer the activity within which certain facts constituted reasons at all. And just as a goal or activity comes to have a place in a man's life, so too can a moral notion. The role of an activity or moral notion in a man's actions appears in the finding of sufficient reason for actions in certain kinds of fact, one of which will *not* be 'That this is a piece of archaeology' or 'This is an act of friendship'. [4]

For Jim, the fact that the villagers had been massacred by Brown was the reason, or 'premise', for concluding 'I must go to the headman' and going. We can ask, therefore, why that was an intelligible reason, and why it was a reason for Jim.

[4] The presence of such a premise in the man's inference would indicate that the agent as form of connection must be explicated by something *other than* 'archaeology' or 'friendship', for example, other goals which have a role in his life.

To answer the first we must bring in the fact that Jim had said he 'was ready to answer with his life for any harm that should come to them if the white men were allowed to retire'. Jim might have provided the fact that he said this as a reason why the massacre of the villagers was a reason for going to the headman. Superficially at least, this would be something like the provision of a major premise in a theoretical inference to show why the minor premise is a reason for drawing the conclusion. The form of connection which provides the intelligibility of these facts as reasons is seen when we locate these statements and the action under certain moral concepts like 'honour', 'friendship', 'respect', and so forth. Turning to the second question, why these were reasons for Jim, we find 'that Jim had such and such a relationship with the villagers' plays the role that 'that A pursues such and such a goal' does in the practical case.

In the archaeological example I gave, neither A's being an archaeologist (pursues archaeological goals), nor archaeology itself entered as reasons into the archaeologist's inference. These play a role in some ways analogous, I have suggested, to that of forms of inference in respect of particular cases of such inferences, and in this sense I have suggested that the agent himself may be seen as a form of connection. If we transpose this to Jim's case, we can say that neither the fact that certain moral notions play a role in his life nor the fact that his projected act falls under these enter as reasons for what he does. The possibility of describing a situation archaeologically or morally is given by archaeology or by moral notions; the possibility of acting for archaeological or moral reasons is provided by the role these play in the person's life. But whereas that role in the case of archaeology can be analysed, I have suggested, in terms of the provision of goals, and hence of reasons both for doing what will attain them, and for a range of non-instrumental acts associated with the importance of the goal to the agent, we have seen reason to doubt whether the role of moral notions can be so analysed. I shall attempt to sharpen this distinction, and show something of the difference which the possession of moral concepts can make to a man's life, in the next chapter, where I shall look at certain possible relations one can have with one's past actions through an examination of the central incident in Conrad's novel *Lord Jim*.

3. Morality and the Past

1. THE EXAMPLE

An inquiry is instigated by the authorities to consider the circumstances in which the steamship the *Patna* was discovered without its white crew and officers. Jim, the first mate, had left the ship with the other crew when it was badly holed by a submerged object. The *Patna* had been transporting a large number of Moslem pilgrims from an Eastern port at the time, and so the danger in which the crew left the ship was not merely a danger to the property of the shipowners, but to human life as well. Jim and the skipper, as officers in charge on the ship, are found guilty by the inquiry of leaving their posts, and lose their certificates. We can say of both of them that they were 'guilty of a crime'. What can this mean? On one level, clearly, it is to be found guilty by an authorized court of law where the relevant evidence has been considered. Certain processes follow immediately on this: sentence is passed and a penalty exacted by the authorities concerned. In this context the question 'what does it mean to be "guilty of a crime"?' is equivalent to 'what is it to be pronounced guilty by a court of law?' But not all questions about guilt can be answered in this way. In particular, such an account cannot apply to the various relations individuals can have to the court's verdict. A man's statement 'I am indeed guilty' is not to be explicated by 'I have been pronounced guilty by the court', any more than 'I am not guilty' means 'I have not been pronounced guilty'. If we concentrate on the two examples of the skipper and Jim we find the difference between a case in which 'I am guilty' would mean 'The court has pronounced this verdict' and one in which it would not. The skipper stands, we could say, in a purely external relation to the idea of his guilt, and the contrast I want to bring out is between this and an 'internal' relation such as we find in Jim's case. The use of 'internal' here is not I think misplaced, for it indicates the parallel to the sort of internal conceptual link we find within the form of connection provided by moral notions with that provided by the agent himself. In this way we shall be looking more closely at the sort of connection there can be between moral notions and that of the self.

2. THE EXTERNAL RELATION TO GUILT: THE SKIPPER'S CASE

The verdict of the court carries with it a sentence, the loss of the certificate which authorizes the holder to command or serve as officer on merchant and passenger vessels. This loss matters to the skipper because of its effect on the prospects of achieving his purpose, an easy, comfortable life. However, these effects are by no means certainly disastrous. They may be merely a temporary inconvenience, and in so far as the wider scheme can still be fulfilled, they can be surmounted by finding an alternative to those positions from which he is now barred. Involved in this idea of an 'alternative' is that of a common measure for assessing the damage caused by the loss of the certificate and the profitability of the alternative proposed. The end in view provides this common measure in terms of which the *relative* seriousness or otherwise of the loss can be estimated. Many parallels present themselves here. Consider the case of failing an examination. The failure matters to the person involved because it means that he does not achieve the desired qualification. In so far as the examination can be retaken, it is possible to regard the failure as a temporary setback. In the event of success, this can be seen as cancelling out the previous failure, for, as far as getting the qualification goes, 'it's all the same in the end'. Once the qualification is achieved, although the fact of previous failure is not removed, the care about it is. The present success alters one's relation to a past event because that relation was determined by the event's effect on the achievement of a goal, and successful pursuit of this is not ruled out by what has occurred.

The skipper is in a similar position. His leaving the *Patna* matters to him because it both removed him from an easy berth and brought the inquiry and its penalty. The terms in which we understand how his act of leaving the ship matters to him are provided by the end he pursued. But this end is not ruled out for him through the consequences of his act, for these consequences do not prevent him from gaining a post where the certificate is not demanded. The seriousness of his action is the seriousness of its consequences, which are assessed in terms of their effects on his achievement of his aim. Now, these consequences follow only through the con- tingencies of discovery, the procedures of the court, and the activities of the ship's owners when employing men to run their ships. Things might have been different: he might not have been found out; the penalties of the court might have been different; officials might have been corrupt; and so on. This context also provides another possibility, that his action on the *Patna* might through the contingencies of what follows be instrumental in getting him a better job. He might through being unemployed happen upon a post offering easier and more comfortable conditions than the *Patna*. He might then bless the day he left his post and incurred the penalty of the court, and that blessing would indicate the increase in profit which occurred due to his loss of the captaincy of the ship.

The loss of the certificate, and hence the verdict of the

court, is bad for the skipper, then, in terms of what that loss may bring in its effects on his achievement of the easy life. The effects, that is, are effects on the means of achieving this end: they matter to the skipper because he seeks this goal. The goal itself provides the terms of assessment for the means or obstacles to its achievement, and in this way the idea of a goal enters into what he does as the provision of reasons for performing actions which contribute towards the goal. The means or obstacles can be efficient or hindering, and it is in such terms as these that we shall understand the notion of the 'best' or the 'worst' thing to do or that has happened to him.

These notions bring with them a particular sense of 'knowledge', 'mistake' and 'problem', concerned with the relation of an action or event to the achievement of the goal. There is room here for the skipper to know that the berth on the *Patna* is likely to be an easy one because the ship is native owned, to be mistaken in this, and to have a problem with deciding which is likely to turn out the easiest job when his life is interrupted by the loss of the certificate. This sense of knowledge goes with the idea of waiting to see if things do turn out badly or not: whether the feared detrimental effects in fact follow. The skipper may *think* the loss of the certificate is bad, but this is consonant with saying 'I was wrong, because things did not turn out as I feared.' The 'best' thing to do in his present predicament is assessed as a way of *remedying* the situation, either in the sense of returning the skipper to his previous position as far as his occupancy of an easy berth goes, or of advancing his interests more positively. The knowledge the skipper might attain by this event in his life would concern the kind of thing to try to avoid in the future. In this sense, the skipper might say that he made a 'mistake' in taking a berth on a ship in a deplorable condition. But what sense could we attach to saying the skipper made a mistake in leaving the ship? He would have reasons for regretting his jump only through the consequences which followed for his pursuit of his goal. If nothing happened, there would be nothing to regret. As the consequences determine the regret in the light of the pursuit of the goal, no regrets are possible in two kinds of situation: where no detrimental effects followed, or where the consequences of not performing the act were more detrimental than those of doing it. Thus, regret is only possible for the skipper because the ship does not sink. If it had, the leap from the ship could not be regretted, for not to have jumped would have meant death, the end of the possibility of the pursuit of his goals. What could have been regretted would have been one's discovery and apprehension. If the skipper regretted the jump, then, this would involve the fact that he *misjudged* the situation: his ends could have been attained, as it turned out, by staying on board. Reasons for regret are provided by the goals pursued in jumping, and to give such reasons will indicate the connection between one's act in its consequences and the pursuit of the goal. 'Why do you regret what you did?' 'I needn't have jumped. The ship didn't sink. And now look at the mess I'm in. It'll be difficult to find such an easy berth again.' Regret for the jump will disappear if the consequences are beneficial; what could be felt would be annoyance at the inconvenience it briefly caused. In other words, regretting the action is possible only if certain effects ensue which are detrimental to the pursuit of one's goal.

What is implied for the self by the judgement 'I should not have jumped over the side' within such a context as this? The 'should not' is explained in terms of the consequences of the act for the achievement of one's goals; the criticism involved is connected with such ideas as 'lack of foresight' or 'lack of knowledge'. But it is also possible to regret jumping and yet disown criticism: 'how was I to know it wouldn't sink?' Here, to regret is akin to cursing one's ill-fortune: 'If only I'd known.' Self-criticism is forestalled by showing that one could not have known what would happen, that one acted as any reasonable man would on the evidence available. To accept criticism is to plead guilty to believing what was on the evidence defeasible. To do so, then, is to accept that one *might* have reached the correct conclusion: one's failure is contrasted with the possibility of success.

Here then we have a cluster of notions which have their life within the purposive perspective. That perspective provides a particular sense for 'knowledge', 'mistake', 'problem', and for 'regret', 'criticism', 'failure' and 'success'. The skipper's act, the leap from the ship, matters to him because of its consequences for the pursuit of his goals. This provides a context in which he could regret his act if, as it turns out, his aims would have been better served by acting differently. If, however, the act was necessary to save his life, he could not regret it, but only, for example, being found out. As the importance of his act is determined by its consequences, a context is provided for such expressions as 'I think this is going to be serious for me', 'I was wrong, things didn't turn out too badly after all', and so forth. The seriousness of the act reveals itself as one learns what as a matter of fact the consequences are. Hence, its seriousness depends on two things: the goals he pursued which provide the standards for assessing the value of the consequences; and, the contingent facts about institutions, the people affected, natural pheno-mena, and so forth, which determine what those consequences are. The 'problem' one has with what one has done is with its effects: it is possible, therefore, to think one will have a problem, and to find that one doesn't. One such problem is deciding on the best policy to pursue now one's life has been interrupted in this way, and here 'best' means 'most conducive to one's ends'. The act itself presents no problem: the problem lies in its effects. The 'mistake' one can be said to have made in jumping runs parallel to the 'regret' one can be said to have: as things turned out, the pursuit of one's goals would have been better served by remaining on board. The 'criticism' involved in such a remark as 'I shouldn't have jumped' goes with this sense of 'mistake': it indicates one's failure to sum up the consequences of the situation correctly. And this indicates that either through luck or foresight, one might have acted 'rightly', where this is successfully predicting the consequences and acting accordingly.

3. THE 'INTERNAL' RELATION TO GUILT: JIM'S CASE

Let us now turn to Jim's case and see if a parallel account emerges. For the skipper, facing the inquiry was irrelevant: it could in the light of his desires, serve no useful purpose. If Jim's case were analogous, we should expect to find an account of Jim's attendance at the inquiry in terms of the advantage he would gain by doing so. Facing the inquiry was important to Jim, but is this an instrumental importance? Let us consider how that importance appears in what Jim says. Having gone over the side of the ship, Jim is horrified at his position. The others, concerned solely for the safety of their lives, row frantically to get clear, beyond the danger of the sinking ship. The thought of suicide occurs to Jim, and his reason for discounting it throws light on how he viewed his situation.

'I believe it would have—it would have ended—nothing . . . No! the proper thing was to face it out—alone.' (p. 97) He explains why this is so to Marlow, the narrator, in these terms:

'I had jumped—hadn't I? That's what I had to live down . . . It was like cheating the dead,' he stammered. 'And there were no dead,' [Marlow] said. 'And that did not matter,' he said . . ., 'Dead or not dead, I could not get clear.' (p. 99)

The necessity for attending the inquiry is closely bound up with that expressed in the phrase 'I could not get clear', and is given explicit form in his reply to the offer of a chance to escape, made to save the white community the embarrassment of a public inquiry into the conduct of white officers.

'I couldn't clear out . . . The skipper did—that's all very well for him. I couldn't, and I wouldn't . . .' (p. 58) In response to this, Marlow tells him:

> 'I am totally unable to imagine what advantage you can expect from this licking of the dregs.' 'Advantage!' he murmured . . . 'I've been trying to tell you all there is in it. But after all, it is *my* trouble.' (p. 113)

Jim's dismissal of the idea of advantage suggests that his attendance at the inquiry will not fall neatly within the proposed model. Jim's reason-giving for his attendance consists, not in the specification of beneficial consequences for his aims, but in a description of what he did on the *Patna*:

> I had jumped—hadn't I? . . . It was like cheating the dead.

This description is followed by the 'conclusion' that 'I couldn't clear out', an inferential situation parallel to that of the example of Jim's going to his death which I discussed above. What we find is that certain facts, that 'I had jumped' or that 'the villagers had been massacred', provide sufficient reason for certain actions, attending the inquiry or going to one's death. If we ask why the skipper did not attend the inquiry we should indicate both that attendance would frustrate rather than aid the achievement of certain aims, and that the skipper had those goals. The 'reasons' the skipper has are given by the specification of the facts about the consequences of so acting: for example, 'that it would result in a delay in finding another job'. The goals themselves are not 'reasons' he has for what he does, but rather provide the perspective within which certain facts become 'reasons' for acting: 'that xing leads to g'. The question, therefore, in Jim's case is what provides the perspective within which facts, not about the consequences of his attendance at the inquiry, but about what he has done, are sufficient reason for facing the tribunal. Just as we as observers would show why certain facts have weight with someone as reasons for action by saying 'He wants x' or 'X is a goal of his', so we should say in Jim's case that these facts have weight with him because 'He feels guilty'. And, just as 'I want x' is not a *further fact* which has weight with me in deciding what to do, but rather indicates my connection with X, which provides the perspective within which these facts can have weight as reasons at all, so 'I feel guilty' or 'I am guilty' is not a further fact Jim considers in deciding what to do, but indicates the perspective within which certain facts become reasons for his actions. In the purposive case the description of the facts which are reasons mention the goal or a further means to it: 'that x' is a reason if it can be expanded into 'That x, and so y, and y is a means . . .', or something of the kind. In Jim's case, the fact 'that I jumped' is not a 'reason' under the description of its consequences for achieving a goal, but under the description 'I betrayed my trust'. This description does not mention 'guilt' in the way a goal enters the description of reasons: 'guilt' enters rather in the fact that to be able *to say and mean* 'I betrayed my trust' *is* to feel guilty and to consider oneself guilty. To feel guilt is to be able to say in morally pejorative terms what one has done.

The skipper's leaving his post matters to him because of its consequences, Jim's because it constituted betraying his trust. The sense in which we can speak of the skipper's 'guilt' is, I have said, an 'external' one. By this I meant (a) that for him to say 'I am guilty' would be no different from his saying 'The court pronounced this verdict'; and (b) that the court's verdict matters to him in terms of the obstacles it places for the pursuit of his aims. Hence, we could say here 'His guilt matters to him' and mean 'The court's verdict matters to him because of its detrimental consequences for the achievement of his desires.' To speak of 'his guilt being important to him' would be odd outside of such an external relation to one's guilt, for in such a case as Jim's to speak of guilt *is to indicate the sort of importance* which certain facts have for him. His guilt is not *important* to him, and not, of course, *unimportant*. What is important is that he jumped, and this importance is brought out by stating this fact in certain moral terms, that he 'betrayed his trust'.

When we speak of the skipper's 'guilt', we do not imply that the skipper sees himself as guilty, and when we speak of his 'betrayal of trust' we don't imply that he could say 'I betrayed my trust'. If he did say this, we should understand him as saying 'I "betrayed my trust". That's what they call it.' We could say, then, that the skipper could not say 'I betrayed my trust' and *mean* it. This sense of 'mean' indicates the role which certain notions play in one's life, whether these be purposive, religious, moral or whatever. In this sense to say and mean 'I want to do x', in most contexts, requires that the notions of certain goals play a role in my life, providing the perspective within which certain facts are reasons for action for me. Hence, whether or not a person can say and mean 'I betrayed my trust' is a quite separate question from whether we can say of him 'He betrayed his trust', for whether he can say this or not depends on the role certain moral notions play in the way he regards his actions.

We followed out the perspective within which the skipper regarded what he had done by indicating how it provided him with a way of assessing the seriousness of his act and in determining on the basis of this what to do. As I have said, the seriousness of Jim's act for him lies not in its consequences for his ends, but in the fact that it was a 'betrayal of his trust'. This fact provides a reason for Jim's remark 'I couldn't clear out' and for his consequent attendance at the inquiry. Such a 'couldn't' relates, of course, neither to a lack of ability (e.g. 'I couldn't clear out because I didn't know how') nor to the relation of the act to some desired goal (e.g. 'I couldn't clear out because Sam Goldwyn will be here on Saturday talent spotting'). Like this last example, however, it does indicate the exclusion of any but a certain kind of consideration as reason for staying, but, unlike it, those considerations do not provide a context for speaking of 'alternatives'. If the starlet knows that another producer is coming to another town on that day, she will have to choose between two alternatives. There being no end in view in Jim's case removes this possibility: 'I couldn't clear out because of what I had done.' The reason is provided, not by the possibility that doing this will lead to something further which might be achieved in other ways, but by a fact about one's past. The alternatives can exist for the starlet because of what her actions may have in the way of consequences: but the consequences are not of immediate interest to Jim. If, however, his aim were a secure job, for example, he might weigh up the advantages of staying, taking the punishment and being accepted back into the fold, or of clearing out. The means for such a comparison are provided by the goal in view. But Jim does not distinguish between staying and clearing out in terms of the advantage of one over the other.

Within the perspective provided by our talk of Jim's guilt, we can identify a sense of 'problem' which relates neither to the determination of any fact about his action, nor to a decision about what to do in the light of its consequences, but rather to the fact that *he* betrayed his trust: 'But after all, it is *my* trouble.' (p. 113) If we spoke of the skipper's 'problem' with what he had done, we should speak either of the determination of the consequences, a problem with prediction, or of a struggle to decide what, in the circumstances, is the best

E

thing to do. Either way, there is something we can call a 'solution'. I want to suggest this is not so in Jim's case. We have seen that he is not concerned in the way the skipper is by the consequences of his act, as possible obstacles to, or vehicles for, his goals. Neither is his problem about the 'facts' of the case, in any clear sense of that troublesome word. Marlow speaks for Jim when he says of the official inquiry:

'Its object was not the fundamental why, but the superficial how, of this affair . . . You can't expect the constituted authorities to inquire into the state of a man's soul . . . Their business was to come down on the consequences.' (p. 42) 'The consequences' of the state of a man's soul are, of course, those actions he performs of interest to the court. About these Jim can tell the court; but this is not what concerns him: 'they wanted facts . . . Facts. They demanded facts from him, as if facts could explain anything.' The court's problem is to determine the facts relevant to the legal apportionment of blame. As such, it is settled by determining that the crew had left the ship in a situation of danger to the passengers and the property of the owners. The guilt established by the court is provided by this finding, and makes no distinction between the skipper and Jim, save in their degrees of authority on the ship. Jim's problem is not to acquire these facts, or, therefore, to establish this kind of guilt. Nor is it concerned with determining the facts about a man's soul which would show why Jim jumped, and which would draw a distinction, irrelevant to the court, between Jim and the skipper. Whereas the skipper had jumped to save his life, that thought, we are told, never occurred to Jim. His act, although it would take us away from the present issues to establish this in detail, was a response to the horror of a situation in which eight hundred people were about to die and the crew were acting in a dishonourable way, trying to save their own lives. His leap is much closer to a flight, or a turning away, from a terrible scene than to a leap to personal safety. The present point, however, is that a sense of 'problem' can be discerned which concerns neither the establishment of the facts the court wanted nor the characterization of his intentions, at least in one sense, for it is very much concerned with the characterization of the act and its motives in moral terms.

Jim's problem is contained in his ability to say and mean 'I have betrayed by trust', in his ability to see what he has done in these terms. It issues not in a solution in terms of a decision about what to do for the best, as the skipper's does, but in that range of actions and thoughts which Jim does and has because of that betrayal. Such acts and thoughts do not stand to the problem as a solution, but as the working out in Jim of the implications of his act for him. With the skipper the consequences of his act determined what it meant for him, whereas for Jim the consequences have what meaning they do because of the moral nature of the act, and, as I shall show in a moment, can be described solely in terms provided by the perspective in which, as we have seen, Jim sees his act. It is helpful in this context to look at the opposite case, the process of excusing oneself, where the fact that one has done something does not present one with a problem in this sense. Here, having or not having a problem with one's actions is being able or unable to describe what one has done in a particular moral way. In any case where an excuse is called for or produced, there is a story of 'how it came about': this story is not at issue between someone who rejects it as an excuse and one who presents it as a justification of his act. As such, the adequacy of an excuse is not the adequacy or coherence of a story. Consider this case. A has said he will attend B's dinner party, but the day before an old friend turns up requiring help. A rings B to say he *cannot* come (which does not merely indicate that two things cannot be done at the same time).[1] 'An old friend I haven't seen for years has turned up, and

[1] Cf. Jim's 'I cannot clear out.'

needs me to go away with him for a time. I know you'll understand if I skip the dinner.' But B resolutely fails to understand: 'You said you would come. Now you say you won't.
You've broken your word.' What is not at issue is the story.
B invited A. A said yes, an old friend of A turns up asking for
help, and A says he will not be coming to B's. Rather, the
issue is whether or no A is justified in so behaving, and that
this is a case of moral justification is shown by B's accusation
that A has 'broken his word'. A's 'excuse' does not show that
he is not failing to turn up having said he would, but that this
cannot, *in this context*, be called 'breaking his word'. He does
this by showing that what he is doing falls under another
moral term, 'helping a friend in need'. In other surroundings,
A would agree that saying he would come and then not turning up would be 'breaking his word'. What A tries to show is
that one cannot in this particular case say, and mean, that A
broke his word; and A himself, of course, cannot say 'I broke
my word'. If A said 'I have broken my word' and meant it, he
would thereby express his sorrow or his sense of guilt; that is,
he would blame himself. The blame is not, therefore, another
detail in the story, but a way of regarding it, a way in which
an agent's actions are important to him.

   Within the purposive paradigm, 'I blame myself' is the
acceptance that one has failed to correctly assess the consequences of one's act's for one's purposes or to correctly sum
up the best course to pursue in a situation. The consequences
of such 'blame' lie in attempts to learn from one's mistakes,
to try to ensure one pays more attention to the relevant
information in the future. The consequences of Jim's blame
appear, not in the determination not to be caught out again,
but in those things he says and does which we can say occur
'because' he acted in this way. Just as failing to assess a
situation correctly, blaming oneself, and determining to do
better, are internally related, so the 'because' here marks an
internal connection. But the implications of the two types of

blame are different. Let me take two examples from Jim's case, one concerned with the way in which he thinks about the penalty inflicted by the court and the other with certain actions he takes, which will serve to mark off this kind of blame from that which we are familiar with from the model of purposive action.

The inquiry brought in a verdict of 'guilty' on the skipper and Jim and ordered that their certificates, necessary qualification for employment with reputable shipping lines, be withdrawn. What, then, are the possible ways of regarding this loss for the skipper and Jim? The skipper regards it, as we have seen, as an unfortunate consequence of his act: as things turned out, his desertion of his post was discovered, and this penalty exacted. For him, the loss is an obstacle to be overcome, by taking a job with a less scrupulous line, by forgery, perhaps, or by some other means. We can hardly provide a parallel account for Jim, even though the consequences of the loss in terms of possibilities of employment are the same. We can indicate the difference by considering two senses in which the certificate could be said to be 'lost'. The first we could call the institutional sense. The relationship between the court's pronouncement of guilt and the loss of the certificate exists because the withdrawal of certificates, like their issue, can only be undertaken by bodies vested with the appropriate legal power. 'Loss' in this context is equivalent to 'withdrawn by the authorities'. The second sense, however, need not bring in a reference to the authorities at all, for it can occur in expressions made prior to any legal inquiry: 'This certificate is lost to me; I am unworthy to possess it.' To mark the difference a hard-headed observer might say 'Of course, he says he's lost it. But *really* he hasn't, only a court can withdraw a certificate.' Where the sense of 'loss' is independent of the institutions of the court, it cannot stand connected to one's act as a legal consequence. Rather, to think about the loss in such a context *would be to think about one's unworthiness*, and hence of what one had done. There is no room here for the distinction between someone who says, when the court orders the certificate's withdrawal, 'I've lost it and that's only right', and someone who responds with 'I've lost it, but so what?' Chester, the West Australian who wants Jim as overseer for a guano-collecting expedition, exemplifies the latter when he says on hearing that Jim has 'taken the matter to heart':

> Then he's no good . . . What's all the to do about? A bit of ass's skin. (p. 119)

The institutional sense is neutral between various attitudes which can be taken to the court's action. The other sense, however, is close to one such attitude, within which the loss is seen as a rightful consequence of what one has done. Within such a context 'I've lost the certificate' could not be followed by 'So what?' or 'So I'll suffer some inconvenience', expressions which have their home in a perspective which judges the seriousness of the loss in terms of its consequences for the pursuit of one's goals. There can be a perspective in which the seriousness of the loss appears, not in its consequences, but in its connection with what one has done. Within that perspective the seriousness of the loss does not wait on developments nor can it be changed by surprising beneficial consequences for oneself. Its seriousness does not lie in its effects, but in what might be called its symbolic relation to the betrayal of trust. If in saying 'By jumping I lost my certificate' I say something whose truth depended on what happened at the inquiry, the 'loss' depended on what, as a matter of fact, occurred. It depended on being found out and brought to trial. For me, it is a matter of fact, on a level with the details of where and when the inquiry was initiated. It is something, however objectionable, which happened to me after I jumped. Against this background, had things gone differently, I could have said, 'Yes, I jumped. But they never found out, so I still have the certificate.' In Jim's case, however, to say 'In jumping I lost my certificate' is not to say something the truth or falsity of which is settled by what occurred after the jump. In the other case, prior to the inquiry, it could be said 'I jumped, so I'll probably lost my certificate.' The loss is something which may or may not happen. My statement is a prediction about what will probably occur. But Jim isn't making a prediction, or a statement which could, with a change of tense, form one. There is no future tense to conjugate 'I have lost my certificate' in *that* context. Rather, to speak like this is to deny the possibility of thinking about what one has done without thinking of one's betrayal of the trust placed in oneself, a connection symbolized in the idea of the loss of the certificate. To say 'I have lost my certificate' is not to remark on the judicial process of the inquiry, but to speak of the betrayal of one's trust, and hence, it is a way in which one's guilt appears, a way in which one expresses the guilt one feels. It is in this way that 'guilt' provides the form of connection between the jump from the ship and thought about the loss of the certificate.

If the way Jim thinks about the court's penalty is different from the skipper's because of the guilt he feels, so are the actions he takes because of what he has done. The acts the skipper performs because he jumped are dictated by his desire for the easy life and the obstacles thrown up to this by the consequences of his act. He acts, that is, to achieve a restitution of his former position, by taking a job with a less scrupulous owner than those from whom he is barred by his lack of credentials. The actions he takes because of what he has done are motivated by the same desires as his taking the captainship of the *Patna* in the first place. For Jim things are rather different.

Let me, then, turn to my second example. Jim's guilt provides the connection between his leap from the *Patna* and his acceptance of a job as a water-clerk after the inquiry. The job, far from being an 'alternative' to the post on the *Patna*, is understood by him in a way made possible solely by his guilt. He regards the relationships involved in this occupation as superficial, and, in a way, corrupt. Conrad tells us that the water-clerk chases custom for the ships' chandlers amongst the captains of vessels visiting Eastern ports. The clerk sails out to meet the incoming vessels:

The connection thus begun is kept up, as long as the ship remains in harbour, by the daily visits of the water-clerk. To the captain he is faithful like a friend and attentive like a son, with the patience of Job, the unselfish devotion of woman, and the jollity of a boon companion. Later on the bill is sent in. It is a beautiful and humane occupation. (p. 3)

The change that is produced in Jim by his guilt is shown by his attitude towards this employment. Both before and after the incident on the *Patna*, he would have said 'This is an unworthy pursuit.' However, before the idea that he should take such a position would have seemed ridiculous: it was not a possibility to be considered. Afterwards, he takes the job as a *fitting* step. It becomes a suitable *punishment* for him, as he sees himself as unworthy and his past life as resting on a false foundation. I shall consider the nature of this change in his life in more detail in the next chapter. What is important to note here is that his taking the job is determined by his *seeing* it *as* a punishment for what he has done. To say this is to indicate that for Jim to think of his being a water-clerk is to think of his betrayal of his trust, for they are related as punishment to a wrong committed. If we speak of Jim's guilt and its consequences we do not, therefore, indicate a species of causal or contingent connection, but those thoughts and actions which are connected to his leaving the ship through the notions provided by the perspective of his guilt. We indicate the consequences of his guilt in terms of the 'loss' of the certificate (in the sense discussed above), the 'punishment' he inflicts on himself, 'facing things out', and so forth, moral notions internally connected with the idea of 'guilt'.

Let us, then characterize the perspective we find here for regarding the past act in contrast with the one described for the skipper. The terms used to bring out the way in which his act matters to Jim do not refer to its contingent consequences for the pursuit of his goals. 'I betrayed my trust' describes the jump itself in a new way, not its consequences. Whether it is of concern to Jim is not to be decided by what as a matter of fact occurs, the ship failing to sink, the discovery by the authorities, the mechanisms of the court's procedures, or the whims of the owners of shipping lines. Nor is its seriousness alleviated by unexpected beneficial consequences. The criticism contained in the judgement 'I betrayed my trust' is not to be explicated in terms of faulty judgement, and neither, therefore, are the associated ideas of the 'mistake' Jim can be said to have made, or the 'problem' he can be said to have as a result. Similarly, what he 'learns' as a result is not something about his mistaken assessment of the situation, but rather that he was someone who could act in an unworthy manner. It is in these terms that the 'problem' poses itself, for it is contained in his perception of his own unworthiness. It is not posed, as the skipper's was, by the consequences of the act, and hence there is no room in Jim's case for the locutions 'I think this could be serious for me' and 'I was wrong, it isn't as serious as I thought'. Jim's judgement that this is serious, unlike the skipper's, implies no prediction about what may or may not happen.

The model of purposive action provides only certain intelligible relations which one can have with an event in one's past. The skipper can regret the consequences of his act, which follow because certain institutions are as they are.

(Recall Hare's remark about the need to change one's moral principles in the light of changes in the social structure due to industrialization or revolution.) Care about the past is care about its effects on the pursuit of one's goals, and hence one's attitude to one's past is always capable of revision as the consequences unfold. Care about one's failures might have been pride on one's successes. Against such a background, Jim's attitude to what he has done and to its consequences becomes unintelligible. The importance of the act is not determined by the importance of its effects, but the effects only have any kind of importance because of the act. The importance of the inquiry is provided by his guilt, the importance of having to choose another job is determined by the idea of punishment, and so on. The importance mentioned here is not that provided by a goal for a fact which can be seen as means or obstacle to it but is indicated in moral terms: the act matters because it was a 'betrayal of trust'. The difference his act made to the skipper was in the provision of new obstacles to the achievement of his purposes, to Jim it meant the provision of a new way of regarding what he had been and the consequent provision of new kinds of reason for doing what he does. It is to the nature of this change that I shall now turn.

4. Language and Moral Change

1. SELF-CRITICISM AND THE IDENTITY OF MORAL JUDGEMENTS

I remarked above briefly that the difference which his guilt made to Jim can be seen in the change which occurred in the way he regarded the job of water-clerk. Before the incident on the *Patna* Jim thought the occupation of water-clerk unworthy and as such it was ruled out for him as a possible field of employment; afterwards, whilst maintaining the view that it is a low kind of job he seeks it as a fitting punishment for what he has done. The 'fit' we speak of here is provided by the unity of his condemnation of both his former life and the water-clerk's existence. We might say, therefore, that what remains constant in the change is the judgement that the water-clerk's job is an unworthy one. But can we identify the two judgements in this way? Certainly, what does not change is the perception that the job involves something akin to the pretence of friendship and devotion for pecuniary ends. But the question is begged by this, for it is equally unclear whether we should identify the talk of 'friendship' and 'devotion' on the two occasions. What differences, then, might lead us to deny the identity of the two judgements on the water-clerk's life?

One is tempted to say that the difference comes out exactly in the fact that Jim after the inquiry calls the job unworthy and takes it as a punishment *for what he has been*. The idea of the punished wrong points back to that life within which the other judgement on the job had its place. In his earlier life to say 'It is unworthy' would be to say 'And therefore unfitting for myself. I am destined for higher things'; the one follows from the other for Jim, in the sense in which, to take a previous example, 'she is old and infirm' may be followed by 'So I'll help her.' In discussing this kind of connection, I introduced the idea of the person as a form of coherence through that of the role which a notion can play in a man's life. When in Jim's later life we find that the very unworthiness of the job is followed by 'So I must take it' we mark, not necessarily a change in the words used to indicate the unworthiness, but a change in the role they, and of course 'unworthy' itself, play in his life. And this is reflected in the difference we can mark between the nature of the *criticism* contained in the two judgements 'It is unworthy', for to use such words is one form criticism can take. In his early life, the criticism of the occupation lay in its contrast with the heroic life, and at that time to make such a contrast was, for Jim, to stress its unsuitability for himself. The criticism in moral terms, the corruption of the job, was connected for him with the idea of the life of the hero, and this in turn was connected with what he thought suitable for himself. Hence, to criticize the job morally was to contrast it with possible occupations for himself. After the *Patna* incident the criticism of the job implies no contrast with what is fitting for himself; indeed, the criticism of the job is part of his self-criticism.

The same kind of thing can be observed if we look at those notions which provided the possibility of the crisis Jim experienced after the incident. Jim could only feel guilty because he had a conception of the duties of an officer, and hence of a trust which he could understand himself as having betrayed. However, the role this notion of trust played in his earlier life was as a necessary presupposition of the heroic, the acting *beyond* the call of duty. As it was not itself a possible subject for heroism, he cared about it solely because the demands of duty must be satisfied if the opportunity of heroism is to arise. Within this context, to think of this trust would be to think of it in contrast to the heroic life, and hence of the contrast between what was good enough for most men and what was the only fitting life for himself. His understanding of his life as dull and prosaic at this time is grounded in the fact that he is only fulfilling his duty as first-mate. In this way, the role of the notion of trust is to provide the necessary contrast with the heroic, and through this the grounds for his dissatisfaction with his present existence. If we consider the situation after the incident, we should have to place it in *contrast* to all this, and relate his thoughts about trust to his guilt at what he had done, and hence to his remorse for *what he had been*. And part of the characterization of his past life would be the indication of the role of the notion of trust there.

2. CHANGE WITHIN THE PURPOSIVE PARADIGM

I want first to consider the idea of this change in comparison with a case provided by the notion of purposive action. I noted in the first chapter that the idea of a goal plays a role in a man's life pre-eminently as a provider of a certain kind of reason for action. One possible kind of change, then, is a change in the reasons one has for doing certain things. We noted, too, that the importance of a goal or activity was marked for someone by his ability to act in certain contexts solely for reasons deriving from the activity or goal. This provides at least two possible kinds of change: the acquisition of new goals, and the change in the importance of an already existent goal or activity. Let us take an example of the latter.

A man looking for a job is offered a position as manager of

a trading post. The company offers it in the expectation of profit, and the man takes it for similar reasons, for he desires to grow wealthy and start his own business. Now, if the reasons for taking the job are limited in this way, certain restrictions are placed on the sort of action which can intelligibly be performed. One sort of action in particular could not be contemplated, which involved the certainty, or reasonable expectation, of death. Within the original terms, he took the job as a means to a further end, and hence as a step within his planned pursuit of a goal. As such, it would not make sense to die for the job, and so defeat the purpose for which it was taken in the first place. If he did perform such an action, we should say that his job had come to mean something more than was contained within the original reasons, and he could be expected to speak of his act in a different way. 'This post is my life. I couldn't run away', for example. Such a way of speaking is clearly different from one in which the relevant considerations are matters of profit: 'I couldn't run away. The company will reward me handsomely for this. It was worth the risk. I could get as much in a day as I could in a whole life's trading.' Within this latter perspective, the *amount of risk* becomes an important factor in determining whether to stay or run, whereas in the other it doesn't.

The acquisition of the new role which his job plays in his life is not merely marked by a change in the reasons for his actions. It is accompanied by other changes. In relation to his original reasons, we can say that he *chose* the job because of the profit it would bring. Where we can speak of 'choosing' other talk becomes appropriate. We may speak of seeing what the job involves for us, weighing up the pros and cons of the alterations it will make in our life. And this indicates that the notion of 'our life' must be distinct from that of the job, for it matters to us only via its consequences assessed in terms derivative from the other goals and activities in which we are involved. But where the original reasons have become inoperative in the way described, this sense of choice disappears, and with it these other ways of talking. We are provided then with a case in which 'our life' is no longer distinct from the idea of a certain activity or goal. We have in this a case comparable with that of Sorel's artists.[1] The value of the activity is no longer provided by its instrumental worth in achieving something further. And this suggests that speaking of 'my life' can be for the individual a way of indicating the role which the notions of certain activities or goals play in his actions and thoughts. This idea is, as I have noted, connected to that of the 'meaning' of activities for a person, and thus to speak of a man's involvement in an activity can be a way of indicating the 'sense' he finds in his life. Such a 'sense' shows in the man's ability to do certain things solely for reasons internal to an activity, not in the provision of external considerations. And, as we have seen, such 'meaning' grows up in the individual's performance of an activity, and so belongs outside the realm of choice and decision. It is something which 'happens' to a man, but not in that sense of 'happens' which indicates a contingent fact about his life, for it is essentially bound up with the very idea of that life at all, and hence with the idea of the person he is. It is not, therefore, something which happens to someone and has great significance for him, but rather provides the terms in which any such significance can be expressed.

3. SIGNIFICANCE FOR THE INDIVIDUAL OF ACTIVITIES AND OF GUILT

This last point indicates the comparison with Jim's case, for we have seen that the change which his guilt made for him was a provision of a new way in which things could have significance. The terms in which the inquiry or the decision to

[1] See above p. 25.

take a job have their importance is provided by the perspective of his guilt. But whereas we can say that our trader finds meaning in his job, we could not say Jim finds meaning in his guilt. How is this reflected in the significance which activities have for each? The meaning the trader found showed itself in his ability to act within an activity solely for reasons provided by it; the reasons Jim has for engaging in any activity, and for his actions within it, derive not from the activity, but from the significance given to it by his guilt. This makes his case look closer to the trader's original situation, in which the value of the job was assessed in external terms. But for him these terms derived from his pursuit of *another goal*, and we have seen reason to deny that 'guilt' operates in this way. It seems that the entrance of guilt into Jim's life marks, not the achievement of meaning in his life, through the meaning found in activities and relationships, but the appearance of a way in which things can have significance which rules out, or limits, the sense in which we can say of Jim that he finds meaning in his life at all. Guilt seems, that is, to rule out the kind of significance the trader's activity can have for him, which I have spoken of as 'finding meaning in his life', without, of course, denying a significance of another sort. And this is indicated by the possibility in the trader's case, but not in Jim's, of indicating the significance of an activity in terms of the 'satisfaction' he gets from it. Such a term is closely allied with 'pleasure' and 'happiness', which too seem inapplicable to Jim's case, and in so far as these terms indicate a way in which the idea of the self can be bound up with that of what is done, we must suppose that another sort of relation is involved for Jim.

We indicate in the trader's case the way the self is bound up with what is done when we show the importance of the activity in terms of his having only certain reasons for his actions. In this way, the role of the notion of a particular activity in a man's life is shown by the way it provides certain 'limits' for what he does. We can isolate three senses of 'limit' here. The idea of the goal makes certain facts intelligible as reasons for action; as a goal of the person concerned, it makes such facts reasons *for him*; and, depending on the importance of the goal to him, it will decide *in cases* of *potential clashes*, which goal, and hence which actions, are pursued.[2] It is also true in Jim's case that guilt makes certain facts intelligible as reasons for action, and as Jim's guilt it makes certain facts reasons for him. The question, therefore, is whether his guilt limits his actions in the third sense; or, in other words, whether the three senses of 'limit' here are the only ones possible.[3] Are the only sorts of conflict a man can experience conflicts of goals, and hence of desires?

Consider one of Sorel's artists, whose lives were a continual striving for artistic perfection, and whose actions within art were motivated purely by artistic considerations. We can envisage one of these giving up work, for no artistic reason, in two sorts of case. In the first, he is tempted from his work by the entrance of other goals into his life, the pursuit of wealth or fame, perhaps. If this happened we should, I think, mark the change by saying that the role of art in his life *had diminished*. In the second, he gives up his work because his mother is dying many miles away and he goes to be with her. Do we similarly want to say here that the role of his art has diminished for him, or that it is not as important to him as it seemed to be? We should not, I think, say that he was *tempted* from his work by the prospect of seeing his mother, nor, if he experienced difficulty in freeing his mind of his artistic problems, would he say there that he was *tempted by art* away from

---

[2] i.e. we have (a) limits on what can intelligibly count as a 'reason', (b) limits on what can be a reason for someone. The latter includes the third sense of limit, for the importance of a goal for a man shows in what he does in cases of potential clashes.

[3] i.e. whether the way in which one's guilt makes certain facts 'reasons' for one shows itself in the way one's pursuit of goals does.

F

his other act. Consider for a moment this latter kind of case. The artist knows he must go to his mother, and that his thoughts should be on her at this time, but finds that his mind remains fixed on his work. He may feel guilt at the very presence of conflict. Now this looks very like a case we do meet with in purposive activities. A man may have problems, not just in his work, but with his own dedication to the activity. Such problems have often provided writers with the very topics for their work. Consider the sort of problem sometimes hinted at in the poetry of Yeats:

> I leave both faith and pride
> To young upstanding men
> Climbing the mountain-side,
> That under bursting dawn,
> They may drop a fly;
> Being of that metal made
> Till it was broken by
> This sedentary trade.[4]

Such problems may be expressed in similar terms to the moral cases we have looked at. The poet may feel he ought to concentrate on his work, and he may feel guilt at being unable to. He feels a desire to occupy himself in other ways, yet feels he ought to be getting on with his writing. Now, unlike the case of the artist, this is a case of temptation, the surmounting of which has a *point* within the art of poetry. A man might be given reasons by others, or may give reasons himself, for conquering his inclinations, in terms of the advantage to be gained by so doing. Unless he does concentrate he will not produce his best work, and so will fail in what he wants as a poet. Perhaps the other desires win and he stops writing, and in some cases we should mark the decline in the role poetry plays in his life by saying that he no longer

[4] 'The Tower' in *Collected Poems* p. 224.

wants to write. In this way we should emphasize the conflict as a conflict of desires, and place this talk of 'ought' and 'guilt' firmly within the realm of the successful pursuit of goals. He will probably fail in his writing unless he ignores these temptations.

Now, if this situation were parallel with the artist's we should have to identify a goal the pursuit of which is hindered by his temptation to concentrate on art. And we should have to identify the effect of giving in to the temptation in terms of its *probable* outcome for the achievement of a goal. If we construed the goal in view as 'being a good son', for example, we should have to see the act of succumbing to the temptation of carrying on with his art as possibly, or even almost certainly, detrimental to the achievement of this. But the connection would be one of probabilities, however high, nevertheless. And hence, even if he gave into the temptation, he might still *not regret it* if it did not turn out disastrously. Thus, the poet might find that giving in to certain temptations did not in fact effect his work, or even that doing so at certain times helped him. But we have noted in one moral case that guilt does not involve care about what is done in terms of the probabilities of any effects, and the same would go, I think, for the artist if he felt guilt at being unable to centre his mind completely on his mother's condition. The relation of concentration on his mother's condition to being a good son is not that of means to end, but rather of conceptual remark to concept. As such, the problem the artist would have would centre on the role his relationship with his mother had in his life, and this, as we have seen, is not the same as worrying about the role a goal or activity plays for him, since in the latter case, *success* in the activity can depend on its playing a certain role. If he cannot dedicate himself he will, *probably*, fail.

4. A Contrasting Moral Case

The change in a person's life due to change in the role played by at least some moral notions is not then the same as that occasioned by a change in the role of a goal. It does not provide a new context for the individual's success, or new ways of living a satisfying life. I want now to sharpen this idea of 'role' in connection with moral notions by considering a way in which an alteration needing a moral description may occur in a life but which does not mark the kind of change I outlined for Jim. For this purpose I shall take the case of the title-figure of Conrad's novel *Nostromo*.[5] Nostromo is chief of the cargadores for the San Tome mine, a silver working in a small and revolution-prone South American republic. Occupants of this exalted position Nostromo regards as 'the rich men, and, as it were, the caballeros among the common people'. (p. 248) Such riches had initially been his goal, but the discovery of his power over men and women and the pleasure of the praise heaped upon him by both high and low, lends a new point to his existence: 'To be well spoken of.' (p. 208) He revels in 'the admiration of women, the admiration of men, the admired publicity of his life'. His actions inspired solely by this desire keep him poor, for this new goal cannot be satisfied merely by the good words of others directed at the normal pursuit of his duties. He gives money away liberally, as 'old or young, they like money, and will speak well of the man who gives it to them.' (p. 208) No longer satisfied to do what he does well, his pleasure in the praise of others leads him to pursue kind words for their own sake. In this form his pride leaves him open to use by others, who can get him to promote their interests in return for flattery. Martin Decoud sees that the Europeans 'make use of'

---

[5] All references to the Penguin edition.

Nostromo (p. 208). Captain Mitchell thinks of Nostromo as 'one of those invaluable subordinates whom to possess is a legitimate cause of boasting.' (p. 48) Nostromo's value is as a tool to remove those obstacles, which the nature of the indigenous population presents to commerce. He helps remove what 'is bad for progress'. (p. 165)

Nostromo, however, imagines that the Europeans' admiration for him is grounded in the way he performs his work, in his power over men. After all, he gives them no money to speak as they do. What does not occur to him is that they value him because of his power, and his power because of its contribution to their goals: he is valued as a tool.

During one of the frequent revolutions, the owner of the mine sides with the defeated party. Nostromo is given the task of removing a cargo of silver from the country to keep it from the enemy. He regards the mission as further evidence of the European's admiration for him:

'What it is to be well spoken of! There is not another man that could have been even thought of for such a thing. I shall get something great for it some-day.' (p. 209)

The way he regards this reward indicates the difference which his desire for admiration has made to him. Initially, he intended to make as much money as possible from his work; he worked to amass wealth. As such, the work, and the good words which accompany it, are valued only as a means to an end. What is of real importance is how much he accumulated for his labours. But there are cases where we can speak of 'reward' where the amount given is not valued for what it can purchase, but for the relation it stands in to the value placed on the service rendered. Here the relevant considerations are not matters of how much the giver can get away with, or the recipient extort, but the gratitude expressed in the gift. We usually think of large amounts of money as expressing deep gratitude, but it can just as easily be imagined here that to receive a 'token' amount from the right person would be to be well rewarded. It is in this latter way that we understand the giving of non-utilizable objects like medals as 'rewards'. And it is in this way that Nostromo looks forward to his reward: he desires a mark that 'not another man could have been even thought of for such a thing'.

The crisis arises when the Europeans use Nostromo to remove the silver from the country plainly with no thought about his safety or future, but in the assumption that he will do what they say if they flatter him enough. This is not, however, the kind of exploit Nostromo would undertake solely for the pleasure of flattery, unless he were sure, as he is, that the admiration stems from a perception of his supreme qualities. As an exercise of his powers, it appeals to him: 'It shall be talked about when the little children are grown up and the grown men are old.' (p. 223) Yet it is not presented to him by the Europeans as if they realized what they were asking of him, but as one more task for a dispensable tool. This fact strikes him, and leads to a period of reflection on his relationship with the Europeans after he has buried the silver and returned in hiding to the mainland. 'The facts of his situation he could appreciate like a man with a distinct experience of the country. He saw them clearly. He was as if sobered after a long bout of intoxication. His fidelity has been taken advantage of.' (p. 344) What Giorgio Viola, the aged Garibaldino, had told him years ago, he sees is true: 'kings, ministers, aristocrats, the rich in general, kept the people in poverty and subjection; they kept them as they kept dogs, to fight and hunt for their service'. (p. 343)

The difference made by this new apprehension of what he has been, a dupe rather than an admired and respected man, is illustrated by the change in his attitude to silver. Previously, the silver had been important to him because of its role in his reputation: not only had he alone been considered capable of the feat of saving it, but the exploit surrounding it was food for legend. The new perception that he has been valued as a servant forces him to alter his view of his reputation, however: he has been famed, not as master of men and lover of women, but as a faithful and guileless servant, easily satisfied by the praise of others. To think now of the silver is not to think of his great and justified reputation for courage and intelligence which will be enhanced by the exploit, but to think of his betrayal by the Europeans and of his own misunderstanding of their relationship with him. From being the greatest exploit in his life it has become the supreme example of his unconscious servility. He feels he has 'inadvertently gone out of his existence on an issue in which his personality had not been taken into account.' (p. 346) The silver, no longer the symbol of the Europeans admiration for his qualities, becomes the only sort of 'reward' he can now take from them. 'He had made up his mind that nothing should be allowed now to rob him of his bargain. . . .' 'I must grow rich very slowly', he meditated aloud. (pp. 412–13) And the fact that the Europeans have no knowledge of the appropriation of their property allows Nostromo to regard his act as one of revenge.

The idea of revenge provides a form of connection between past and future: the harm done to one is repayed. The nature of this transaction depends on what is seen as appropriate retribution, and this often involves, as in Nostromo's case, the turning of one's harm, understood in one set of terms, to one's advantage, understood in another. Thus, Nostromo turns the harm he has received, the indignity of being treated as a servant, to his advantage, the accumulation of wealth. The connection thus forged between his riches and the indignity provides for ways in which the idea of revenge can play a role in his later life too: in the pleasurable recall of how he duped the Europeans, in the connection between the riches surrounding him and the bitterness of his memories, and so forth.

The change which occurs in Nostromo's case obviously depends on those notions which give rise to his thoughts of revenge, and which provide, therefore, the terms of contrast between his imagined regard by the Europeans and the reality he now perceives. These are to be found in the ideas of those qualities Nostromo feels he possesses and which are the subject of his pride: his power over men, his attraction for women, his courage and intelligence. Thought about these is for him connected with contempt for others who are seen as lesser beings. It is to this range of connection we point when we say that they are at the centre of his pride. He imagined the Europeans admired him for these qualities, but finds they valued him above all for his tractability, as a good servant. His pride remains undiminished, and its hurt is alleviated in the plan of revenge. He has discovered the unworthiness of others, not of himself.

The difference between his and Jim's case lies, therefore, in the difference between the sorts of change which can surround the two judgements 'They are unworthy' and 'I am unworthy'. We can indicate these differences in several ways. Thus, we might say 'He is unworthy, and I put such trust in him', whereas if I say 'I am unworthy' I don't mean that I have betrayed a trust I placed in myself. If I trust other people I expect them to do certain things, and if they are trustworthy I am able to predict they will in fact do them. But if I say 'I trust myself to . . .' I mark, not the placing of a trust and an expectation about behaviour, but an intention or determination to carry something through. We could say that 'I expect him to . . .' or 'I trust him to . . .' contains both a moral (for we will blame him if he fails) and a predictive element. The first person phrases, 'I expect/trust myself to . . .', on the other hand, contain a moral and an intentional element, and in this they share the same kind of difference as that between

'He intends to . . .' which is based on evidence, and 'I intend to . . .' which is not. 'He is unworthy' marks the acquisition of conclusive evidence: 'I suppose I suspected it, but it was finding him actually taking the knives from the sideboard that clinched it . . .' 'I am unworthy' marks, not the attainment of evidence, but the achievement of a new role for certain notions in one's life. If I realize his unworthiness, I no longer expect him to behave in certain ways. When Jim realizes his own unworthiness, he does not realize he no longer can expect certain behaviour from himself. On the contrary, the realization changes what he intends to do and hence his behaviour; if it didn't, it could be doubted if he had in fact been able to say and mean 'I am unworthy'. It is this which leads us to say that the change which occurs when I realize X's unworthiness is, not a change in me, but in what I know, whereas the change which occurs when I realize my own unworthiness is a change in myself. It is because of this that 'He is unworthy' can go with 'It has been a bitter blow to find this out', whereas 'I am unworthy' could hardly do so. It is difficult to make sense of the idea of one's discovery of one's own unworthiness as an occasion for disappointment, even though one might say 'I wish I had been better.'

To apply certain moral terms to oneself is to feel guilt or to blame oneself, and this obviously does not go for their application to other people. The achievement of guilt or remorse is marked by the presence of new intentions and new reasons for action, and it is this sort of change I have spoken of as a change in the role played in one's life by the moral notions contained in the first person judgement. But it is not just the provision of new reasons and intentions which is at issue, for that goes for Nostromo too when he discovered the true nature of the Europeans admiration: it is rather the relation in which the new stands to the old. In Jim's case the point of speaking of a new role was to indicate that the new *called* in *question* the old. Indeed, the very raising of a question

G

about the role certain notions played for him marks a change in the role they play, and the new role develops from this through the processes of guilt and remorse. The possibility of being able to say 'I am unworthy' marks the start of such a process, whereas no third person judgement can by itself call in question the role certain notions play in one's own life (although it might be a stage on the way to being able to make the first person judgement). The first person judgement itself, in other words, marks a change which the third could not.

5. LANGUAGE AND CHANGE

I want now to consider briefly some of the implications of my account for philosophical discussions of what has been called 'the language of morals', and in particular, to ask whether orthodox discussions of 'the meaning of moral terms' can cope with the sort of alteration in Jim's life we have considered. When we speak of the change in Jim in terms of a change in the role certain notions play in his thoughts and actions, we indicate such things as the following.

(i) To say a person is unworthy is no longer to give a reason for avoiding him. In this respect we could compare Jim's behaviour towards the *Patna*'s crew before the incident, and that towards the ship's chandlers and their employees afterwards.

(ii) To say an occupation is unworthy is no longer to see it as ruled out for oneself. Here we could look at his attitude to the water-clerk's job.

(iii) Before the incident, to think about his past was to feel dissatisfied: it consisted merely in performing what was required of him by his position as first-mate. His past lay contrasted with a future of heroism for which he is in constant 'preparation'. After the incident, the dissatisfaction, if we can use this word here, embodied in looking back arises, not from the frustration of his desires, but from the perception that those desires had led him to behave unworthily. The topic of this moral criticism is the life within which that other criticism, and its attendant notions of unworthiness, falseness of relationship, and so forth, had its place.

(iv) That i–iii in part explicate what it is for Jim to be able to say and mean 'I betrayed my trust', and hence, 'I am unworthy'.

Now, when we ask whether someone 'knows what a moral word means' we may decide in the affirmative in the face of any of the following, depending on the situation. This does not mean, as we shall note in a moment, that these are alternatives.

(i) The provision of a dictionary definition: ' "unworthy" means "having little or no moral worth".'

(ii) The provision of a group of further moral descriptions, one at least of which must usually be applicable to justify the use of 'unworthy': ' "Unworthy" conduct is such things as dishonesty, betrayal of one's trust. . . ." '

(iii) The provision of examples of acts, described non-morally, which fall under both a required moral description and the term 'unworthy'. ' "Betrayal of one's trust" is unworthy conduct, and by this I mean to include such things as abandoning one's post as a ship's officer to the danger of passengers and ship, but not, for example, spying on one's own country for another if one strongly disapproves of the social or political system of one but strongly approves of the other. I know some people do speak of betraying one's country, and do so in terms of trust, but I cannot see it in this way.'

The ability to engage in the sort of explication and argument found in (iii) is presupposed by the idea of giving a dictionary definition or verbal formula. (Those who can produce formulae alone are said to have 'learnt by rote', and hence not to know what the word really means.) Ability to engage in this sort of discussion is the ability to apply the term in question in particular cases. We emphasize the idea of application when we say that the person must be able to say and mean remarks of the form 'X's conduct was unworthy'. We do not say and mean definitions or formulae in this way. To say and mean 'X's conduct was unworthy' *is* to disapprove of it, and we should expect certain other kinds of talk and behaviour to go with the remark if we are not to withdraw the claim that it is really meant. To know what a word means is to be able to mean something when one uses it, not merely in the sense of uttering words which have meaning (that is, could be used by others to say and mean something), but in the sense of being able to follow through its implications in feeling, word and action. And to say this is to say that the notion in question makes a difference to what one says and does, and hence to point to the role the notion plays in one's life. Thus, the idea of the application of a term, and therefore of its meaning, leads to that of the role it plays for an individual, and so, in the case of moral terms, to those considerations I have been concerned with in this essay.

Changes in this role do not always appear straightforwardly in the provision of definitions, formulae, or examples, for that is only one part of the role notions can play. In Jim's case, for example, the same definitions or examples could well be given by him both before and after the *Patna* incident. Such explication is a specialized business, and is only one aspect of the role these notions play for Jim. The role is not exhausted by the provision of examples and formulae, nor by our ability as observers to pick out from his talk a satisfactory range of cases. We can look elsewhere to fill out this role, particularly to the sorts of problem and action it makes possible for Jim. These will, of course, appear in what he says and in what others say about him, but not if the focus of our interest is on whether he can satisfy conditions i–iii above.

To understand those conditions we must understand the

idea of the application of the term concerned, and this will lead us to consider the nature of the criticism or disapproval contained in that application. And it is there we located the sort of change we find in Jim's, rather than Nostromo's, case. Or consider the way one can in later life regard earlier relationships, and what this can show about the connection between the two periods. A young girl, whose notion of love is nurtured by the reading of romance novellas, has a relationship with a boy which would, in its problems and the way it dies out, be unintelligible without this background. Later in life, she may look back and think how shallow the relationship was. This criticism was not open to her earlier self, for the understanding from which it emerges was attained *only through* the process of disenchantment with her earlier affair and what that made possible for her. But the difference between the 'shallow' relationship and the understanding which issues in this criticism will not appear if we ask if she knew what 'love' meant in her youth, in the sense in which that can be answered through i–iii above. In another sense, of course, we do say that at the earlier period, she did not know what 'love' meant, but by this we are not indicating an inability to satisfy those conditions. Nevertheless, a change has come over her life, intelligible only through the idea of 'love' which is marked by her ability to say and mean 'I love him' at that time t^1 and 'I didn't really love him; that was not love at all' at time t^2.

We say that p excludes -p, for the one is the negation of the other. We say that a man cannot consistently hold both, although as a *matter of fact* he may. The case of 'I love him' said at t^1 and 'I didn't really love him, I didn't know what "love" meant' said at t^2 differs on at least two counts from this. They are not contradictories, for the latter involves a temporal reference the former lacks. They cannot, as a matter of fact, be 'held' at the same time, for the temporal reference excludes this possibility. But clearly the sense in which time 'excludes' is not that in which p excludes -p. If I say 'p' at time t¹ and '-p' at time t², I may criticize myself for saying 'p': but the possibility of saying '-p' was contained in my saying 'p'. But 'I didn't love him. I didn't know what "love" meant' can criticize the self by criticizing what was meant by 'I love him' said at the earlier time. We have here a sense of 'meaning' tied up with the idea of the self. In the other case, the criticism of the self proceeds not by indicating the inadequacies of what one was able to mean but through other considerations: the use of the wrong techniques, carelessness, and so forth. (Compare the difference discussed above between the criticism of the self possible for the skipper and for Jim.)

It is characteristic of the moral theories I began with to take as a starting point a certain view of meaning which excludes taking seriously examples like these. Consider, for example, the notion of language underlying Hare's moral theory. Meaning, Hare tells us, 'of any kind (so far as it is *words* that are said to have meaning) is or involves the use of an expression in accordance with certain rules'. (*FR* p. 7) Different kinds of word have different sorts of meaning-rule. Thus a descriptive word like 'red' has a descriptive meaning rule, and 'a descriptive meaning rule is one which lays it down that we may apply an expression to objects which are similar to each other in certain respects'. (p. 13) We can express this by saying 'Everything like this (pointing to a red object) in the relevant respects is red', where for 'like this' we can substitute 'a term which describes the respects in which the thing in question is being said to be like this. If no suitable word exists, it is always possible to invent one.' (p. 11) Moral words differ from descriptive ones in that, because their function is to guide conduct, their descriptive meaning rules become principles of conduct. Such an account settles for an analysis of the problems surrounding the 'meaning' of moral terms through definitions. Apart from the problems peculiar to Hare's account, the sense in which words can be said to 'describe' respects in which things are similar, and the idea of 'inventing' terms and so on, what is ignored is the essential matter of what it is to apply moral terms, the role they play in men's lives. It is perhaps because of this that it is assumed the important questions connected with the idea of application can be answered in terms of the role purposive notions play. It is easy enough to ignore the problems posed by this move if one begins one's investigations with a word like 'red' (or in Foot's case, 'round' ('Moral Beliefs' p. 83[6])), for provided a person can recognize red when he sees it, and this is one of the earlier capacities we develop, we will usually say 'he knows what "red" means'. Here those other problems about meaning do not easily arise. We say 'she knows what the word "love" means, but she doesn't know what love is', but not 'she knows what "red" means, but she doesn't know what red is'. Such a distinction points to those processes of change, of development and recession of understanding, if you like, characteristic not merely of moral terms, but also of certain notions associated with the purposive activities, within which terms like 'red' or 'round' have their sense. Where such processes are missed, morality itself is lost to inquiry.

6. CONCLUSION

The central problem of moral philosophy seems to me to be how we should identify and describe the importance which moral considerations can have for a man. The continuing attempts within contemporary philosophy to answer the question 'Why should I be moral?' stem from a perception of the importance of this problem, although they seek an

[6] In P. Foot (ed.) *Theories of Ethics*, Oxford, 1967.

answer by locating the significance of morality within that of purposive activity, and, therefore, I think, go wrong.

We raise the question of the importance of certain kinds of consideration when we inquire into the connection between reasons and actions. Within such an inquiry, two kinds of question arise. (1) How are these particular facts intelligible as 'reasons' for this kind of action? Such a question will lead us to speak of the nature of the activity (archaeology, art or whatever) and of its problems, methods of work, and so on. (2) How are these reasons intelligible as 'reasons for' the individual concerned? This question is directed towards the examination of those notions which link the idea of the self to (in the case of purposive examples) activities and their related goals. Within this class of notions, we identified not only the more usually treated ones of 'wanting', 'intending', and so on, but also that of the 'meaning' a man finds in what he does, the 'significance' it has for him. Such meaning shows itself primarily, although not exclusively, in the absence of external reasons for actions within an activity, and is therefore connected with that relation between the self and an activity we indicate when we talk of 'being an archaeologist', 'being an artist', and so on. The identity indicated here marks the role which certain kinds of goals, problems, and their associated reasons for action, have in a man's life, and marks thereby the 'meaning' one can find in one's life. This latter phrase indicates that involvement in an activity can provide, not merely a perspective within which certain facts are seen as reasons for actions, but one which contains a more general sense of the importance of things for a man. We see this in both its provision of a way of regarding what happens to oneself, death, injury, and the contingent consequences of one's involvement with the activity, and in the possibility of *non-instrumental* action stemming from one's relation to the activity. We find here the intelligibility of a man dying 'for' his activity, as well as the more mundane cases arising from the respect, care and dedication of a man for his work. Such cases involve the use of certain locutions having a use also in moral cases: 'I ought to do x' and 'I must do x', which cannot be explicated in instrumental terms (that is, in the way we should describe 'I must/ought to do x if y is to be achieved'). However, as these locutions issue from the place certain activities and goals have in the man's life, they do presuppose the idea of those activities and goals. A range of notions, including 'care', 'respect' and 'dedication' are associated with such first person remarks. These notions indicate, not further reasons a man has for what he does, but the role which certain kinds of reason have for him. They relate, we could say, to the perspective of the self in its involvement with an activity, and are not contained within it. X's care for his subject is not an additional reason he has for doing A, but shows itself in his ability to do A for certain kinds of reason.

The significance we speak of in talking of the role an activity plays for someone provides a sense of 'problem' which is not to be identified with a 'problem in the activity' ('an archaeological problem', for example). Having a problem about one's dedication to archaeology is not a seeking for an archaeological solution. The 'problem' issues rather in such things as an intention of determination to try to concentrate wholeheartedly on what one does, or in the fading of the importance of the activity for the individual. That is, in changes in the role which the notions associated with the activity play in one's life.

The closeness of such problems to ones we identify as 'moral', as well as the use of a non-instrumental use of 'ought' and 'must' in both contexts, marks moral notions as closer to those concerned with a man's relation to an activity than to those of the activity itself. They are closer to the notions of 'meaning', 'care', 'respect' and 'significance' than to those of 'goal' or 'means'. Moral notions I have suggested mark, not something which can assume an importance for a man, but *a kind of importance* which certain facts can have for him. It is this which is lost in asking 'why should one be moral?', for any answer to this must show how moral considerations are *given* importance rather than the kind of importance they embody. This also shows why those cases in which moral considerations are *given* an importance can be the subject of moral criticism (cf. Gwendolen). Thus, just as 'significance' or 'care' mark an importance which certain kinds of fact (those of goals, and means to them) can have, so 'charity', 'honour' or 'guilt' mark an importance which another range of facts are capable of. Unlike those notions concerned with a man's relation to an activity, the facts given importance do not derive from the activities which the man may pursue. We have, therefore, the dual problem of indicating both the range of facts concerned and the nature of their significance. The latter concerns, as in the case of the man's relation to a purposive activity, the connection between the self and what is done. As it does not presuppose goals, it will not go, as 'care' or 'dedication' do, with the idea of their successful pursuit, or the 'satisfaction' or 'pleasure' which often can substitute for the talk of the 'significance' or 'meaning' found in what one does. Indeed, in so far as moral notions indicate a kind of importance which certain facts can have, those notions associated with the importance of purposive activities should lie ill with them. As we saw, to speak of the 'pleasure' or 'satisfaction' (or their opposites) derived from acting morally, is to identify what is done within another sort of context, to remove the possibility that the reasons for what is done derive solely from moral notions (cf. Nostromo).

This introduces the distinction between an internal and external relation of the self to moral notions. We noted that in the case of 'practical' reasoning within an activity, we can distinguish between those facts taken as 'reasons' for the action concerned, and that which makes them 'reasons', or

the 'action' what it is. Consider an example, 'If the composi-
tion of the picture is to achieve balance, a darker colour is
needed here' followed by an action specified by 'putting a
darker colour in this area' and thereby as 'trying to achieve
compositional balance', said and done by a particular individual. Both 'reason' and 'action' require for their specification
artistic terms, and hence presuppose the practice of art. But,
in so far as the fact 'that if compositional balance is to be
achieved, x must be done' is a 'reason for' the individual, we
are led to consider the different question of what is involved
in seeing this fact as a 'reason for' someone. Here I suggested
the notion, not of the practice of art as a form of connection
within which certain facts can count as 'reasons' for action,
but of the agent as form of connection within which certain
facts constitute 'reasons for' an individual's actions. Neither
the practice of art nor the role artistic notions play for the
individual enter themselves as facts constituting reasons, for
that would require other forms of connection within which
they could count as 'reasons'. This enables us to distinguish
between what I called an 'internal' and 'external' relation of
the individual to an activity. Where a man stands in an
internal relation the fact that 'Xing is a piece of art/
archaeology/etc.' does not enter as a reason for the performance of the action concerned. This 'fact' specifies, rather, the
form of connection within which the man has his reasons for
his actions. Where it does enter as a reason itself, then we
look for some further form of connection, in terms, for
example, of a further goal or activity pursued, within which
that fact can be constituted as a 'reason' and 'reason for'.
And there, *those* forms of connection, indicated by facts of
the form 'Xing is doing Y' or 'Y is a goal of individual I' cannot themselves constitute reasons. Thus, to take a not too
bizarre example, someone whose aim is to be accepted by an
artistic community for the purposes of sociological inquiry,
would have as a reason for his actions in painting, or

whatever, what an artist never would, 'that doing this is doing "art" '. And this points to that distinction between someone whose actions are solely to be described in artistic terms, and someone whose actions are to be described as 'doing what counts as "art" '. A man's involvement in an activity comes out in the absence of such reasons.

The same sort of distinction can be found within the moral cases we have considered. We can distinguish between a man who takes cognisance of moral considerations for ulterior purposes and one who does not, and this is marked by the presence in the case of the former of the fact 'that xing is "charitable"/"honourable"/etc.' as a reason for the action. We can, therefore, distinguish between the sorts of consideration which would allow us to say of someone that they knew what the term 'charity' or 'honour' meant, which would be common to both of these cases, and the role which such notions play in the actions of the individuals concerned. As in the purposive example, the paradigmatic case on which the other's possibility is parasitic is where that role appears in the absence of ulterior motives. Hence cases where the fact 'that xing is charitable, etc.' marks, not a reason the man has for what he does, but the sort of fact which constitutes reasons for him, are paradigmatic for morality.

We began by distinguishing between the form of connection provided by an activity and that provided by the agent's involvement in it. But, as the agent's involvement is exemplified by those cases in which we speak of someone as *really* moved by 'artistic reasons' or 'moral' reasons and these are ones characterized by the presence solely of 'artistic' or 'moral' reasons, we see that, from the point of view of the agent, there is no distinction here, for neither are reasons which he has for what he does. And this indicates something further about the notion of 'externality'. The terms indicating the involvement of the individual, 'X is an artist' or 'X is charitable', have a primarily third person usage, entering into explanations of why X does what he does, and not into X's reasoning about what to do. A similar thing could be said about statements of the form 'doing a is to do "art" ' or 'xing is called "charitable" '. Where such facts can play a role as reasons for action, the agent stands in a similar relation to an activity or morality as an observer.

Similarly, whereas the importance which goals or activities have for an individual can be indicated by the observer in terms of 'care' or 'dedication', terms not deriving from the goals or activities themselves, that importance is seen from the agent's point of view *in* the goal or activity itself. What is lacking in moral cases is the applicability of a range of expressions not deriving from morality for indicating such importance, notions, that is, parallel to 'care' or 'meaning' in the purposive case. Moral notions can enter a man's actions in such a way that it becomes inappropriate to describe the importance to himself of what he does by bringing in the sort of individual reference contained in expressions like 'He gets great pleasure from xing' or 'Xing is his whole life.' And this is connected, as we have seen, with the way in which moral considerations provide a 'limit' to what a man sees himself 'able' to do, where this term cannot be explicated in terms either of the possibilities provided by an activity or those of the agent's involvement in it. This directs us to consider the ways in which moral considerations can override, and provide a new perspective on, purposive ones. And this points to the other side of that problem I suggested as central in moral philosophy, the nature of the importance moral considerations can have for a man, namely, the way the notion of the self, and therefore of a man's life, is connected with that of morality. The deepest difference between purposive and moral ideas will appear in this.

Index